Ronnie Gilbert
on
Mother Jones

Ronnie Gilbert on Mother Jones

Face to Face with the Most Dangerous Woman in America

Ronnie Gilbert

Conari Press
Berkeley, CA

Printed in the United States of America on recycled paper
Cover: Sharon Smith Design; photo: Mark Avery

Black and white photos of Mother Jones courtesy of The Archives of Labor and Urban
Affairs at Wayne State University (p. 44, 80); The Charles H. Kerr Publishing Co. and The
Labadie Collection at The University of Michigan at Ann Arbor (p. 8); Underwood and
Underwood and The Labadie Collection (p. 42); and The Library of Congress (p. 6).

ISBN: 0-943233-48-8

SPECIAL NOTE ON SONGS
The songs in this play are also copyrighted. Information on how to obtain the music
for the songs can be had by contacting Abbe Alice Music, PO Box 8388, Berkeley, CA
94707.

Library of Congress Cataloging-in-Publication Data

Gilbert, Ronnie.
    Ronnie Gilbert on Mother Jones : face to face with the most dangerous
woman in America / Ronnie Gilbert.
        p.   cm.
    Includes bibliographical references.
    ISBN 0-943233-48-8 : $9.95
    1. Jones, Mother, 1843?-1930—Drama. 2. Labor leaders—United States—
Drama. 3.Women in trade-unions—United States—Drama.
    I. Title.
PS3557.I34226R6   1993
812'.54—dc20   93-17099
                                                                        CIP

Permissions

For Donna

and in memory
of my mother

Contents

Acknowledgments   1

Ronnie Gilbert on Mother Jones   7

"Mother Jones:
  The Most Dangerous Woman in America"   43
    Act One   45
    Notes on Act One   72
    Act Two   81
    Notes on Act Two   113

Bibliography   119

About the Author   123

Acknowledgments

Mother Jones' published speeches and letters can be found in two volumes by Edward Steel and one by Philip Foner. Foner's also includes newspaper interviews, journal articles signed by Mother Jones, and her verbatim testimony before Congressional committees. The Charles Kerr Company, the oldest socialist publishing house in the U.S., keeps her autobiography in print. I am greatly indebted to all these, which I referred to extensively in researching and building the play.

Of the three Mother Jones biographies published in the 1970s, the most useful to me was Dale Fetherling's *Mother Jones: The Miners' Angel.* Other valuable references were the autobiography of Florence Jaffray Harriman and a publication of *Goldenseal Magazine* called *The Goldenseal Book of the West Virginia Mine Wars,* edited by Ken Sullivan. Essays on the labor movement by Foner and on the woman suffrage movement by Gerda Lerner, Bettina Aptheker, and Aileen Kraditor aided my understanding of Mother Jones' position on those issues, which I raised in the play.

I used Mother Jones' own words wherever possible, and invented when it seemed advisable and I was so inspired. The intention was to entertain and inform, but never to distort Mother Jones' point of view for the sake of theatrical expediency. I hope the words I put in my character's mouth sound as if they came from the original and that in other ways I have been true to her. But we're left with the fact that my understanding of the truth of Mother Jones is just that—my understanding, an invention, too, of a kind.

As to the writing of this play, my first, I had all kinds of help, and I want to acknowledge it.

Larry Lillo, the Vancouver Playhouse's artistic director, walked with me from the very first pages, reading, critiquing, suggesting until there was something to work with. I am deeply in his debt for the skill and time he gave to this project.

Maureen Heffernan was at a first meeting when I had quite a different play in mind. Later, as this one was developing, she came and helped me sort out the pieces, find out where I was.

As artistic director of the Milwaukee Repertory Theatre, John Dillon booked me and "Mother Jones" into the Stackner Cabaret on faith, and when I arrived with a work-in-progress twice as long as the cabaret could accommodate, he helped me cut it down to size. Some of those cuts in fact were quite salubrious, I have since found. (He also dubbed me "Playwright," for which I will always love him.) Sarah O'Connor provided, magically and graciously. Kate Henderson designed a beautiful set for the tiny space, and Dawna Gregory designed the costume. Norma Saldivar was "Mother Jones'" champion. She plunged into the material with enthusiasm that matched my own, fought for time and won some, too. It was also a pleasure to experience the intelligence and style of her direction. Romulus Linney said Hurray! and gently suggested where the ongoing writing work needed to be. He was so right.

As this book goes to press, the Berkeley Repertory Theatre is about to give "Mother Jones" her first full-scale production under the direction of Timothy Near, artistic director of the San Jose Repertory. The script, which is the one in this book, is quite different from the cozy vehicle it used to be. Ms. Near worked with me to revise it, an effort that had the generous attention of the Berkeley Rep's artistic director, Sharon Ott.

As a singer with access to concert audiences, I had unusually fine opportunities to try different approaches to the material of the play. For their cooperation and hospitality, I want to thank: the Freight and Salvage Coffee House in Berkeley, the Ark in Ann Arbor, The Eighth Step in Albany, The Turning Point in Piermont, NY, and producers Ellen Friedman in Cambridge, Kendra Kopelke in Baltimore, Tracye Lawson in Santa Cruz, and the Walkabout Clearwater group in New York. These come to mind; there may have been others, no less important to the process.

When at last I saw I had a workable play, Donna Korones, my manager and the executive producer of the project from the start, called together a group of friends, and they were its first audience: Margie Adam, Julie Bennett, Jill Davey, Nancy Duff, Mollie Katzen, Joan Miller, Shane Miller, Mary Jane Ryan, Pam Shepard, and my daughter Lisa Weg, offered thoughtful and insightful responses. Ongoing conversations with several of them, as with Carole Johnson, Joan Lester, Jan Montgomery, Marya Grambs, Si Kahn, Nan Fink, and Susan Griffin (who also helped pry me loose from a stuck place) were greatly helpful, especially on the issue of Mother Jones' paradoxical attitude towards women. Feminist philosopher and educator Elizabeth Minnich offered an analysis in a phone conversation that was particularly illuminating in that regard.

A few weeks after the Milwaukee engagement, I repeated the performance at the Sheldon Concert Hall in St. Louis. As Walter Gunn, the Sheldon's executive director and Michael Killoren, the program director, foresaw could happen (and worked hard to accomplish) Mother Jones and I became the catalysts for bringing together as an audience two groups that usually have a hard time finding one another, the labor and women's communities. It was a genuinely inspiring experience for me.

Light and sound technician R. "Tag" Parker did magic with minimal technical resources (they've been upgraded since) and the Sheldon's very willing staff, and he later contributed his skill for a single performance at the Folly Theatre in Kansas City.

A word about the songs: in all this testing of material before various audiences, the one sure thing that didn't ever need testing was Si Kahn's songs. They were wonderful as soon as they were finished and a great treat for the audience even while the play was in transition. Si Kahn is a visionary people's poet with an awesome capacity to take ideas and information given in the most pedestrian language and return them as songs of great beauty and power. And he is fast! This play is especially blessed to have his compositions.

Although the music for the songs does not appear in this volume, I want to thank the musicians who have worked with me on it: Libby McLaren did the first piano arrangements and played for me in all the pre-Milwaukee work; John Bucchino demonstrated what a consummate musician/arranger using an electronic synthesizer could do with some of the tunes; it was then that I stopped kicking and screaming and decided to enjoy what is left of the 20th century. Jack Forbes Wilson scored and arranged the music and played for the Milwaukee engagement and later for the Kansas City performance; his lovely presence on stage, as well as his exuberant musical artistry, made performing with him a real pleasure for me. In St. Louis, Linda Presgrave learned the show and took hold of it (in not a lot of time) and was a fine and sensitive musical partner. Keith Hughes will be the musical director for the Berkeley Rep production.

Others to whom I am indebted are Jackie Alper, Jude Binder, Peter Fowler, Jeff Langley, Jane Lurie, Lois McLean, John Moffatt, Emma Ware, Barbara Morland at the Library of Congress, Les Orear at the Illinois Labor History Society,

Jim Wolfe of the Sylvis Society, Richard Reynolds at *Mother Jones* magazine for access to their files, and Penelope and Franklin Rosemont of the Charles Kerr Publishing Company.

Ann Shepherd, dear friend and first theatre mentor, came to Milwaukee to check out my first venture as writer/actor. She left me with actor's notes of brain-tingling brilliance, reminding me once again of what drew me like a magnet to her and to theatre in the first place, thirty years ago.

Mary Jane Ryan and Julie Bennett of Conari Press were at that first play reading in Donna's and my living room. In the play and the discussion that followed, they heard the possibility of a book and proposed it. Ah, thought I, another excuse to indulge my obsession with Mother Jones. And I have all those leftover notes from the play; what a snap. Hubris! It wasn't a snap at all! But Julie was determined, and editor Mary Jane cheered, instructed, and coaxed an essay out of me, much to my surprise. I am very grateful to her for her skill and patience.

I wish also to thank the Windcall Resident Program for four beautiful weeks of care and quiet in the hills of Montana, which got me started.

I've saved for last the one who is really first, my life partner Donna Korones, manager extraordinaire, who fuels the project and has done so since the beginning. Donna never settles for anything but your best, and hers. It was she who sponsored my three years of study and writing; she who envisioned the role of our community and engaged them, whereas I would have stayed cooped up in solitary; she who moved the play out from behind the computer and into performing position; and she who continues to provoke, prod, protect, analyze, organize, and lead the way.

Ronnie Gilbert on Mother Jones:

Face to Face with the Most Dangerous Woman in America

Mother Jones: The Most Dangerous Woman in America was about three years in the writing and development; more, if I count from the beginning of the reading and research time, and, of course, a play goes on being reworked in one way or another as it is played. But the preparation for it really began long ago, in my childhood, quite literally at my mother's knee.

Like Mother Jones, my mother was a unionist and a socialist. In her way, Sarah Gilbert shaped her life as Mother Jones had—actively, around dearly-held political principles: unionism, anti-racism, economic justice for all. As a child, I understood my mother's example this way: Brushing your teeth twice a day and working for social justice are necessary for good personal hygiene.

So when I started reading about Mother Jones' life, I felt I understood her. Her working class identity, her social values and beliefs were very familiar to me; I still share many of them. Simply and fundamentally stated, they are that a sane, just, and humane social system places life well above property rights, and that despite the difficulty in doing so, the human race has the capacity to create such a system and keep it in place. (However, Mother Jones, at least in her public utterances, was more optimistic than I about humanity's will to do so.)

However, it was "on the woman question," as my mother used to say, that I differed most strongly with Mother Jones. She was a nineteenth century socialist and as such, believed that socialism would transform human society and behavior and then women would automatically rise to a higher place. I believe that women had better take a higher place now or society will never be transformed; in fact, it may very well succeed in destroying itself.

Still, I could develop Mother Jones' negative stance on female suffrage in the play, because I understood it even while disagreeing with it. A more difficult challenge was to understand the woman behind the monumental life, lived for more than half a century in the belly of the shark. The woman behind the brave, witty, repetitious, and frequently contra-dictory rhetoric that sometimes seemed to have come from the sensibilities of a nun and sometimes from those of a street fighter. And finally, to understand the woman whose perplexing contrariness toward women and the women's movement of her day caused her to be rejected by current feminists searching history for powerful role models.

To understand the woman, the private person behind the public figure, you have to find her. With Mother Jones, there's the rub. For Mother Jones is a cipher. When she died in 1930, she left behind millions of words: articles, speeches, interviews, official public testimony, even an autobiogra-phy, all of it about the fierce and loving matriarch of the working poor—her public persona. But the words tell us next to nothing about her personal life, the personal life of the woman, Mary Harris Jones.

The autobiography disposes of her family of birth in the first paragraph: Her father, Richard Harris, emigrated from Ireland to the United States, brought his family over, and then moved them to Toronto where Mary was raised as an American citizen and went through the common schools and attended the Normal. There is no mention of a mother or siblings.

The second page says she married "a staunch member of the Iron Moulders' Union" and gives a brief and moving description of the Memphis yellow fever epidemic in which he and their "four children" died. Neither his name nor the children's were mentioned. And that is it for personal information.

No siblings, no lovers, no close friends in Mother Jones' life? Yes, she had a brother, William Harris, dean of the Archdiocese of Toronto, a published writer himself. How do we know? Only because a eulogy for him, clipped from a Catholic magazine, was found among her few papers when she died. Evidently, he never wrote about her, either.

She did have friends. Her book says, "I went with a friend," "I opened a business with a partner. . ." "A friend told me. . ." Who were these people? She never said, and biographers have not yet been able to fill in the gaps.

If the paucity of personal material is frustrating, so is the questionable accuracy of what little there is. For instance, on the matter of husband and children: twenty-five years before the autobiography, it was three children she mentioned to reporters, not four. A West Virginia woman declared that when she was a child she heard Mother Jones speak of an only son who died at age nine or ten. A mine union organizer who knew Mary Jones was sure that her husband had been a coal miner and had been killed in the mines. Why the differing stories?

One thing Mother Jones was never reticent about was her age. It popped out of her declarations like chewing gum bubbles, as in: "It took six of Gov. Peabody's lap dogs to take me, a woman of sixty-five, and put me on a train to get me out of the country." Or: General Chase "had better go back to his mother and get a nursing bottle. He'll do better there than making war on an 82-year-old woman in a state where women vote." Very good. But look at the dates. The first statement was made in 1904, the second in 1914. In 1909 she said she was seventy-four, and in 1910 she claimed to be seventy-six. This means she was born in 1839 or 1832, 1834 or 1835, take your pick. One writer even suggests she may have been born as late as 1843. That would have made her only eighty-seven when she was celebrating her 100th birthday!

Of course, it is quite possible that Mother Jones never had more than the foggiest notion of when she was actually born; many families in her time made no particular fuss about birthdays. As long as she was choosing her age, she could turn other people's ageism to her advantage, couldn't she? An old gray-haired woman might just as well be eighty-two as seventy-five and be seven years more impressive. . . .

A particularly nice touch was the coincidence of Mother Jones' stated birthday happening to fall on May first. May Day is militant Labor's great day, celebrating the struggle for the eight-hour workday and honoring the martyrs in that bloody struggle. Mother Jones had been deeply involved in the Eight-hour Movement and so it is only fitting that her birthday fell on that day.

It would be unkind and untrue to conclude that Mother Jones was a liar; for the most part her stories were corroborated by witnesses (in one form or another). Instead, I would say that she was one of that talented breed of great storytellers who would never let the absolute truth spoil a good yarn.

Her life as a union organizer was full of danger and close calls, as she faced down governors, generals and gunmen; her only ammunition her courage, her wit, and her rhetoric. Whenever she worked out a clever strategy or got off a humorous barb at an enemy, the story went into her basket of triumphant goodies, regardless of how the battle itself actually went, whether it was won or lost. These tales were pulled out and retold again and again in her speeches and testimony, with impressive transformations in the retelling.

To Mother Jones, that basket of swashbucklers was probably infinitely more interesting than stories of her family life. Only recently have women been encouraged (mostly by other women) to see something worth talking about in the dailiness of their lives. For Mother Jones, the details of years with her family might have seemed too ordinary to mention. They might have been too painful, as well. But I would love to know something of what made this woman who she was. Her father was a laborer, probably with pick and shovel, on the railroads and canals. Did he prosper? Is that why she could go through school instead of spending her youth in domestic service, the fate of so many immigrant Irish daughters whose parents had to lighten the burden of feeding large families on small incomes? Was it a large family? Who was her mother? What was their relationship? What about religion and politics; what place did these have in the early life of this woman who lived a life of such adventure on the one hand and self-abnegation on the other? Writers have conjectured, but we don't know.

Such a total blackout of a public figure's personal life, especially such a controversial public figure, would be hard to achieve today, when everything is fair game for interviewers, so that the public can know all, down to one's brand of deodorant. But even considering that hers was a more reticent age, it seems strange that in thirty years of interviews, into the last weeks of her life, no one could get her to talk about anything but social issues.

Unless they didn't ask. Did it never occur to anyone to connect an old woman with a personal life other than a stereotypical cookie-baking, baby-bouncing granny, which Mother Jones was clearly not, though she dressed the part?

Long after Mother Jones was dead, more than thirty years afterward, the woman who edited her autobiography, who may have done much of the actual writing of it, was quite alive: Mary Field Parton lived well into the 1960s. Apparently, no one thought to ask her what she knew of Mother Jones, whether there was anything more to her life than what appeared in print.

But suppose someone had looked at Mother Jones as a woman. If it were me, an interview might have gone this way:

RG: Mother Jones, what about that photo of you and Terence Powderly on a garden bench, the good-looking gent with the beautiful white moustache?

MJ: What photo, let me see. Oh, yes, isn't he handsome. . .

RG: You look extremely coy in that picture, Mother Jones. See the way your head is tilted, your hand turned out, the little smile—almost simpering, if you don't mind my saying so. Did you have a thing for Terence Powderly? Were you lovers?

MJ: Nonsense! Terence Powderly was my very dear friend, I knew him for forty years. I practically lived in his house, in fact, I did live in his house whenever I was in Washington. They kept a room for me, he and his wife Emma. In fact, even after he died, she took great care of me when I was ill.

RG: I see. Well, I could have sworn. . .

MJ: Well, you would have been wrong.

RG: Not even in the old days, before he became Grand Master Workman of the Knights, when you were youngish people going to the Knights' picnics?

MJ: I was older than him. And I'm not going to answer any more questions about Terence Powderly!

RG: Okay, don't get your dander up. Let's just say you were unusually serene the day of the photo. But wasn't there anyone else, then? I mean, an intimate friend, a lover, male or female?

MJ: What! Don't be ridiculous, how could I keep lovers,

traveling constantly, on the moment's notice, sleeping wherever I could lay my head down?

RG: Elizabeth Gurley Flynn was an organizer; she managed to have love affairs. Emma Goldman. . .

MJ: Oh, well, Emma. . . . No, my work was my love. "My boys" were who mattered to me, "my children," the exploited workers of America. . . .

RG: Yes, yes, Mother. But I'd still give a lot to know who you kicked up your heels with all those years.

MJ: Well, you're not going to find out! I didn't answer those bastards who said I was a whorehouse madam, and I'm not going to answer about my love life. In my day we didn't talk about such things. It was private.

Private or not, the 1904 charge by the Denver anti-union scandal sheet, *Polly Pry*, claiming that Mother Jones had once been a sex worker had been picked up by newspapers all over the country; it dogged her for years. Whenever the United Mine Workers were involved in serious disputes, the scandal against her would be revived—how better to get at the union than by turning their famous organizer, their stereotypical Madonna, into a stereotypical Whore.

During the 1914 Colorado coal wars, a congressman from that state with connections to mine-owning interests actually read the material into the Congressional Record. This brought forth a furious protest from the normally conservative Terence Powderly in which he vouched personally for Mother Jones' engagement elsewhere during the time in question and excoriated the congressman for using the record "to assail a white-haired, aged, defenseless woman." John Mitchell, the UMW president, however, who might at least have been expected to exercise a little gallantry on behalf of his valuable colleague, had nothing more to say than that he didn't know her in those days. *He* wasn't going to get involved. Sue them if you like, but leave me out of it, seemed to be his stand on the issue. It couldn't have enhanced her opinion of him.

As for the "white-haired defenseless woman," she took the union attorney's advice and let the charge go unanswered. And so it remained. Some years later, writer and fellow Socialist Upton Sinclair said she told him that the whole thing stemmed from her having once berated the Catholic diocese in Chicago for refusing to bury a prostitute in its hallowed ground. Then again, she is said to have told a friend, "Don't you think whatever my past might have been that I have more than made up for it?"

If there were some truth to a "shady" past (there is a long period of pre-organizing time in her history, though not the time of the charge, that is as yet completely unaccounted for), Mother Jones would have been a vulnerable target for scandalmongering by political enemies. In that case, the best course might very well have been to treat all of her personal life as privileged material and keep the trail hard to follow. The juggling of dates, the lack of information about her Toronto family, and the absence of any indication of contact between them could be explained that way.

But of course this is pure conjecture; there could have been any number of other reasons for an obsession with personal privacy. Suppose her immigration and citizenship status through her father was shaky, for instance. A serious family rupture over anything—politics, religion, or a personal falling out—could account for the lack of contact with family. There could actually even have been some correspondence, lost in the constant relocation of her personal belongings, often mentioned in her surviving letters. Or, like most women until recently, she may have been convinced that her own personal pre-organizational life was not interesting, not worth talking about. We don't know.

But my strong feeling is that at the point in her life when Mary Jones became "Mother" Jones she locked into that persona and played it for all it was worth. She costumed herself appropriately, with long black skirts and lace-collared shirtwaists long after even poor women her own age had given them up. Looking closely at photographs, you can see that her getups were at least partly homemade. Mary Jones had been a professional dressmaker before becoming a union organizer. If she had chosen to update her wardrobe, she could have easily done so. But the costume was part of the persona, and a great one it was: everyman's fantasy mother of that time: the gray-haired defenseless old sweetie they wrote all those syrupy songs and flowery speeches about. Her persona not only got her down into the mines past a lot of murderous guards, but onto the stages of a hundred theaters and hallowed auditoriums, into the White House and the presence of forty years' worth of chief executives.

It even got her past the cynicism of certain smart newsfolks, like the *New York Times* reporter she managed to bamboozle in 1913. Expecting the "blood-red flag, incendiary talk in uncouth English," the writer got instead reasoned, "mild-mannered sociology." Clearly dazed, this reporter, he or she, wrote in a long, often-quoted feature story, "She has a powder puff. That, too, astonished me. . . . If she be, in truth, a Doctress Jekyll-Mrs. Hyde, she is as wonderful in her black silk, her carefully dressed, silvery hair, her silk stockings and neat pumps, as Steven's male doublet is between the covers of his book."

How did Mary Jones develop this extraordinary political savvy, this sophisticated capacity for pulling out of herself just the right measure and tone, for being just the right sort of "Mother" for whomever was her audience?

Her enemies were never successful in penetrating the disguise, in turning the picture around, even with attacks on her virtue. It was an image that sealed itself against puncture like a good tire.

A harmless mother to the media where it served her well,

she was true Mother to the dispossessed, not "dear old Mother," but Lion Mother, Bear Mother, Warrior Mother, battling for the souls of her "children," shaking them awake from the torpor induced by enforced poverty and ignorance to get out there and fight.

When I read her words and imagine her, I think of the African-American mothers and grandmothers of today battling to raise responsible, healthy children up out of the hell of the inner cities; I think of single mothers—Welfare Warriors, some call themselves—learning to wring blood from a stony system, fighting with any means possible to keep their children with them, under a roof, and decently fed; I think of lesbian mothers battling tooth and nail against a homophobic society that would rip their children from them; I think of my own mother and her contemporaries in the 1930s and 40s, all day bending over the roaring power sewing machines, rushing home at night to cook and clean and oversee children. Immigrant women, they were, Yiddish- and Italian-speaking—nowadays they're Asians and Haitians and Latinas—pushing their children past the roadblocks—a bigoted teacher, an indifferent administration, a flawed curriculum: Learn! learn!

Mother Jones was in their mold, no matter how many children of her own she did or didn't have. The day-to-day struggle of the mining town mothers was her struggle, their urgency, hers.

"Four of [my children] died with whooping cough, all at once. I was working nights and nobody to do for them, only Myrtle. She's eleven. . . . So I had to quit my job and then there wasn't any money for medicine, so they just died. . . ."

This all-too-common story was Ella Mae Wiggins', North Carolina millworker, songwriter, and unionist (quoted in *America's Working Women*) And this is her song:

We leave our home in the morning
We kiss our children good-bye
While we slave for the bosses
Our children scream and cry.

To come into an industrial area with a message about improving working conditions through unionism in those days when the Robber Barons and their spawn ruled industry was indeed a dangerous business. Nowhere was it more dangerous than in coal mining country and no coal areas were more dangerous than the beautiful and isolated hills and hollows of Colorado and West Virginia, the scenes of some of Mother Jones' most impressive battles.

Labor accounted for most of the cost of mining coal, so there was maximum profit for the owners as long as wages were kept low, and low they were kept, by any means necessary, beginning with a Catch-22 system that kept miners and their families literally in peonage to the owners. The last line of Merle Travis' famous song "Sixteen Tons" sums it up neatly: "I owe my soul to the company store."

Aside from the mine itself, the most profitable enterprise in a coal town was the company store, the "pluck me," as it was commonly called. Here mine workers and their families were forced to buy all their food and provisions, from clothing to the blasting powder the men used in their work, at shamefully inflated prices. The bills that piled up at the company store were in fact calculated to exceed a worker's paltry income; he might never see actual cash in the year.

This, plus exorbitant rates charged for the company-owned shacks the families were forced to live in, and a series of other regular raids on wages, kept the people in perpetual debt. If a miner was killed or disabled, his family was expected to work off that debt. This system of locked-in debt was standard in the industry, a great aid to maintaining a working population trapped in poverty and dependent on whatever the company was willing to pay in wages. It meant enormous profits to the corporate owners.

Obviously, such a system of exploitation required a system of protection: revolt was always a potential threat. The companies fortified their holdings. "Protection" agencies, such as the hated Baldwin-Felts Detectives, specialized in taking care of mine property and "troublemakers." Some areas became so perilous for union organizers that the union had trouble finding men to go in and organize. This was the vacuum that Mother Jones often filled for the UMWA. "You could do the most good in the Fairmont field," President Mitchell wrote her in 1902. "The companies up there have evidently scared our boys, and of course with good reason, as they have brutally beaten some of them. I dislike to ask you always to take the dangerous fields, but I know that you are willing." *The miners' angel,* as she was called, plunged in where others feared to tread. She held meetings under the very noses of the detectives, sometimes actually daring gunmen to do her harm. Somehow they never managed it, although some tried.

One writer conjectures that in the face of such violence, Mother Jones may have owed her safety and success to her age and her sex. I think it's a fanciful notion. All women in an atmosphere of violence were at risk, then as now. Hired gunmen, sheriff's deputies, sent out to evict strikers' families from their shacks kicked, clubbed and beat women and children. Police and soldiers were no respecters of femaleness.

A case in point was the fate of a lively but peaceable demonstration in Colorado of strikers' wives and other female supporters. They had come out in orderly parade to protest the jailing of Mother Jones by the military. There were babies in arms; small children were along. Mounted militia-men were also there, supposedly to keep order. Their commander was mild-mannered optician John Chase, now in his alter-ego as Brigadier General Chase of the Colorado militia. At some point, General Chase accidentally backed his horse into a cart, the horse began to buck, and the General lost his seat and fell off. This amused the women, who had a mighty laugh at the poor fellow's expense. Furious, the great man remounted and ordered his men to charge. They did, sabres drawn. Women and children were knocked to the ground, trampled, one had an ear nearly severed. There's certainly plenty of reason to suppose that her gender renders a woman even more vulnerable to violence among violent men.

Mother Jones was under no such illusions about her vulnerability. One day, a friend saw her gazing at a picture of Mrs. Fannie Sellins, another UMWA organizer, like herself. "Whenever I look at the picture of her," she said, "I wonder it's not me lying on the ground."

Mrs. Sellins had been helping out in a steel strike, as Mother Jones had done herself from time to time. Armed guards in the employ of the steel company shot Fannie Sellins and smashed her skull in, in full view of women and children. And Ella Mae Wiggins—she was murdered by mine guards in a strike at Gastonia in 1929. No, a sweet face, gentility, and age were about as much protection then against men intent on enforcing their will and wielding their power as they are today, as hundreds of thousands of rape victims and battered wives through the century can attest.

Mother Jones probably owed her success and safety in the field to two other factors instead, both well-known to today's guerilla fighters. One, she maintained absolute solidarity with ordinary working people; women, children, and men hid her when she was in enemy territory, spied for her, and kept her moving ahead of the posse. Even imprisoned, she made allies, as when she recruited a young guard to help her get a message out of a military jail where she was being held incommunicado.

Two, she had a matchless instinct for getting herself and what she was doing into the news, bathed in public light. Thus, the message below was addressed to Senator Kern in Washington, D.C., who was even then trying to get the Senate to investigate West Virginia mine practices. The next day, Senator Kern read Mother Jones' message to the entire U.S. Senate and press corps:

"From out of the military prison wall of Pratt, West Virginia, where I have walked over my eighty-fourth milestone in history [Here, she's born in 1829!] I send you the groans and tears and heartaches of men, women and children as I have heard them in this state. From out these prison walls, I plead with you for the honor of the nation, to push that investigation, and the children yet unborn will rise and call you blessed." It's good, isn't it?

Dramatic telegrams, oratory heightened with dashes of poetry, music, demonstrations and processions were her stock in trade. Put Mother Jones in front of an audience, she was in her glory, with a voice that could be heard (before microphones) indoors or out at the very last row of spectators, a voice described variously as soft and mesmerizing, high and sweet, deep, powerful and shrill. Give her a moment of danger, she played it to the hilt.

According to a miner who claimed to be there, Mother Jones, in a one-horse rig, led a column of striking miners toward an unorganized coal camp "to do business," as she called it. Suddenly, they came up against a group of mine guards with machine guns, blocking their way. Mother Jones looked over the scene, calmly drove the rig up to the gun emplacement, was helped down, walked up to one of the machine guns, patted the muzzle and said to the gunman behind it, "Listen, you. Fire one shot today and 800 men in those hills will not leave one of your gang alive." They were allowed to pass. Later, Mother Jones admitted that if there were miners in those hills, she knew nothing of it. "I

realized we were up against it, and something had to be done,"
she said, "so I pulled the dramatic stuff on them thugs."

Mother Jones loved this episode and told it often with
embellishment, though one would hardly think that was
necessary. The yarn well represented her stated philosophy:
"I'm against violence—I like drama."

One might imagine that Mother Jones would be an icon
for the women's movement of our time. In fact, contemporary feminists looking for strong role models have passed her
by or given her bad reviews, and this is because of her
surprisingly negative attitude towards the women's movement of her own time.

For although Mother Jones may have taunted General
Chase with the power of the Colorado women's votes,
sounding for all the world like a militant suffragist, the fact
is that she opposed woman suffrage right down the line. She
simply gave herself the right, in a battle, to use any verbal
argument that might be effective. (What other weapons did
she have in the battle?) She'd stand up in front of thousands
of tough men and prod them into action by calling them
cowards and threatening to bring women in to show them
how to fight; she informed a Congressional committee that
one woman in Congress would clean up the mess in the
country; speaking like a dedicated feminist, she once
declared, "As soon as every woman grasps the idea that
every other woman is her sister, then we will begin to better
conditions," and, in a dig at President Theodore Roosevelt
and a congressional commission, she smirked, "You fellows
do elect wonderful presidents. The best thing you can do is
to put a woman in the next time. . . ."

Yes, she believed women were fighters and had power
they themselves hadn't discovered. But when it came to
voting, her position, quoted in the *New York Times* and
every newspaper that interviewed her was: "In no sense of
the word am I in sympathy with woman's suffrage. In a long

life of study of these questions I have learned that women are out of place in political work. . . ."

Of all the seeming paradoxes in Mother Jones' public stances, her opposition to an organized movement of women trying to empower each other is the most difficult to comprehend. She kept up a running battle with the suffrage movement, sometimes resorting to sarcasm which delighted a press that had its own anti-suffrage, anti-women's rights agenda. Picturing Mother Jones as an enemy to women and to women's concerns was useful, a way of getting two birds with one bullet, and she gave the newspapers plenty of ammunition. Not surprisingly, some of the feminists of her time, as limited in their own view as she was in hers, judged her "androcentric," concerned only with the interests of men.

The facts of her life, however, show that Mother Jones was actively interested in women and women's concerns, and it seems to me that it is a kind of tunnel vision to continue to see her that way today, when we can see her and those issues in retrospect. If I could speak with her about this now, perhaps the conversation might go something like this:

RG: I don't get it, Mother Jones. What did you have against the suffrage movement? Why were you such an anti?

MJ: I was not an anti-anything that could bring freedom to my class, the working class. The suffrage movement was a movement of moneyed women. They had no interest in the problems of the working class, and I had no interest in them.

RG: That's a pretty broad statement—no suffragists had any interest in the working class. What were Susan B. Anthony and Elizabeth Cady Stanton doing at the 1868 convention of the National Labor Union, the first national conference of the first national federation of unions in American history?

MJ: Tsk! . . .I know what the NLU was! William Sylvis was my George's hero, for god's sake. Sylvis helped organize the NLU. Worked himself to death, he did, first pulling all the iron molders into a national, then organizing all the other unions into a federation. Sylvis and the NLU, Sylvis and the NLU. That's all George talked about for months on end, the National Labor Union. We didn't make it to the 1868 convention. George died the summer before.

RG: Yes, I'm sorry. But you must know, since you knew William Sylvis, that he was a strong and outspoken advocate of women's rights and universal suffrage.

MJ: Yes, I know, I read and heard about the convention. William went to bat for Mrs. Stanton when the delegates didn't want to seat her. Well, it's understandable they didn't: she was from a suffrage and not a labor organization. And then William praised her, said she had done more than anyone he knew to elevate her class and his too. And they did seat her, even though they voted against setting up any official connection between the NLU and woman's suffrage. And that was right. The NLU couldn't afford to split over that issue.

RG: Do you know that when Mrs. Stanton described that convention she wrote, "The country would be safe in the hands of these labor people?" She said that the discussions at the convention—and I'm quoting her—"were superior to those of any body of statesmen ever assembled on this continent." It seems William Sylvis wasn't the only labor man who understood the need for woman's rights.

MJ: Yes, well. . . Sylvis would have dropped dead if he had heard Miss Susan B. Anthony the very next year at the labor congress explaining how she sent a bunch of women in to replace the strikers in a typographical strike so that the women could get experience in the industry. As it was, poor William dropped dead before the Congress, so he didn't hear it, and a good thing, too. Imagine! Scabbing for work experience! And you think she ever admitted the error of her ways? No, she prints in her newspaper, "The worst enemies of Women's Suffrage will ever be the laboring class of men." Why didn't she say that almost half the laboring class of men at the Congress understood the women's problems and would have let her sit but they were outvoted, and fairly outvoted? After all, she violated a cardinal principle of unionism, and in all her explanation, she didn't seem to understand that at all. Well, between Miss Susan B. Anthony's strike-breaking and the death of poor William Sylvis, we didn't hear much about woman suffrage for quite awhile.

RG: What a shame. That would have made quite an alliance—labor and woman's suffrage. . . . What a lot they could have learned from each other. Maybe with labor's support, the vote would even have come a lot sooner, and when it finally came, what a coalition for progress!

MJ: Ach, you're dreaming! What have you been drinking?

RG: You don't think oppressed women and exploited labor could make common cause?

MJ: One, all those European miners and steel mill workers did not want their women voting. It would have taken a major campaign to convince those men—yes, and plenty of the home-grown boys, too—that they'd still get their sausages cooked and their shirts washed even if their wives learned to vote. Two, your high class ladies of the suffrage movement were not yearning to soil their white gloves shaking the grimy hands of the working poor. It was none too good when they did get together. With exceptions, of course. Now, Jane Addams was alright, I'll admit. But what about the rest of them, turning against the Negro, and then against immigrants and then Labor in general. They start off saying "Universal Suffrage! Let all human beings without exception have a say in who makes the laws they live under." Fine! And then all of a sudden, it's no longer all human beings, it's only white human beings and native born human beings, and then it's only those who own property, and then only those who can pass certain tests.

According to your suffragists, we poor were ignorant, drunk, and corruptible; whereas the women of the upper classes were pure as the driven snow, ready to vote the proper way—to keep the rotten system as it is! What did that Carrie Chapman Catt say? "The Government is in danger from the male vote in the slums, and the ignorant foreign vote; the miners are watching with greedy eyes to despoil the wealth of the country." Greedy eyes!

Come on, why would I speak for the vote of snooty ladies who brag that if given the vote they will keep out anyone sympathetic to labor? They said it themselves, the suffragists. That was their selling point: the votes of the suffragists would ensure defeat of the "undesirable elements." No. I wasn't going to support that! There were enough upper class male voters standing on the necks of the poor without adding women's dainty boots, as well.

RG: Mother Jones, you know perfectly well that wasn't the whole story. Within the suffrage movement there were all kinds, including labor women. Wouldn't it have been wonderful if those laboring women had had you to support their point of view in the movement. You always said it was important to work for change from within a mass movement. . . . And I feel strongly that personal contact with you would have gone a long way to open the minds of some of those women.

MJ: Listen, darling, I didn't have time. There was always a strike breaking out somewhere. Men were being shot and women, too. Children going hungry, barely surviving. It was life and death. I know many of those suffragists meant well. But they had the time to play around. It was a different world that we lived in.

The world of the mining towns was a different world even from the working class world of the cities. Life in the vast mine fields of the country was still nearly feudal in character, and in those days before television, before even radio, the outrages against human life, especially against the life of women, were hidden from the awareness of those who lived far away, even those who knew the hardships of life for the urban poor under monopoly capitalism.

It was to the nearly invisible women of this hidden world of rural poverty that Mother Jones gave her heart, the thousands of weighed-down women of the mountain mining towns of Pennsylvania, West Virginia, Illinois, and Ohio in the east, and Colorado, Utah, and Arizona in the west. Although Mother Jones traveled the country frequently, speaking in the great cities to huge audiences, cheering and inspiring their women factory workers with her appearances during their strikes, her closest alliances and her deepest concerns were with these mountain women whose shacks she slept in and whose scant food she shared. These women she nursed when they were sick, and helped care for their children. These women she held in her arms when a child died or a husband was killed. In strikes, she found food for them from neighboring farmers, collected money and clothing for them wherever she went, and organized them into enthusiastic and effective battalions of picketers and scab dousers.

She never pitied poor women, as the well-meaning suffragists tended to do when they discovered the poor. As a working class woman herself, she furiously resented the attitudes of privileged superiority, *noblesse oblige*, that engendered those feelings of pity. She knew the power and pride, the defiant resourcefulness, the robust joy in life and the extraordinary faith of poor women, native or foreign born. Constantly, she challenged her male audiences with women's strength, militancy and endurance. She challenged women, too, to appreciate themselves that way: "This is the fighting age. Put on your fighting clothes. You are too sentimental!"

Flatly, she proclaimed: "Women are the foundation of the nation. No nation can rise above its women." She meant it, believed it with a passion. Her ideal, the well-read, intellectual working class woman, needed only adequate economic support to become a reality. It was a basic socialist idea, and millions of people throughout the world were turning to it: solve the economic problems and all else will follow. (In her lifetime, there had not yet been an experiment to prove or disprove the theory.)

But the poor woman's reality, the world she lived in, was not about theory, it was about life-threatening emergency: this day's food for the table, this winter's coal for the stove and shoes for little bare feet; this week's anxiety about the reported rumbles in the mine that could be signaling one of the horrible accidents that killed the men and overnight left women and children destitute.

This reality was completely different from that of the leisured women of the suffrage movement. Like her upper class sister, the poorest, most abject working class woman might yearn to be a professional instead of a mill worker, or to partake of the world of the mind, might ponder the questions of identity and self-worth and personal fulfillment as she labored. But labor she did, to exhaustion, in those times, and for many, in these times, too. The unmarried factory worker or "working girl" might sometimes choose hunger in exchange for something to read, for the pleasure of a concert, or in our times perhaps a movie. But if she had children, she would not choose starvation for them. The book, the concert, the suffrage meeting would have to wait.

And here was the great difference: that the poor woman, once she became a mother, was part of a family to which she was quite literally bound, while the leisured woman, although she depended upon her husband for support, could, by virtue of his spending ability, leave the small, loved tyrants in some hired someone's care for a time, and be true to that yearning self, or at least fight for the right to be true to it. But the working class wife, as Gerda Lerner wrote, "was and is essential to family survival," as well as being bound to her husband for her own survival. The family could not survive without her (unpaid) labor, her children could not survive. This Mother Jones was acutely aware of.

Poverty was the enemy, and those who created it. Poverty bolstered the child labor system, ripped children from their mothers, forced them into factories, into the mines, grew them up ignorant, trapped in a never-ending cycle of ignorance and more poverty. Poverty forced mothers out of their homes to work in the mills, as today it forces so many poor women into underpaid factory or service jobs or into hours of housecleaning for the financially secure. Where were poor children to get their supervision, their care and training as human beings and future citizens, if not from their mothers, Mother Jones asked. Public child care for the poor? There was none. "Sorry, Judge, but miners' wives can't afford nurse girls," said a young West Virginia mother who brought her crying babies with her (at Mother Jones' suggestion) during her arraignment for harassing scabs.

What was talk of voting and the right to a career to Mother Jones, who knew that the dearest wish of such a woman was a decent house with running water and indoor plumbing? Fault her for not seeing the possibility of good public child care, which could have freed both mother and child? Today, nearly a century later, we can hardly afford to feel superior on that score. Where is our good public child care to liberate mothers and children?

Did the suffrage movement address itself to the needs and rights of these women, and these children? It did not. In fact, it became a strict policy of the suffragists to avoid at all costs "side issues" which might split women into factions and divert them from their long struggle, their ultimately single-minded goal of obtaining the vote. For Mother Jones, the ability of middle class women to speak of women's rights and at the same time ignore the often desperate plight of huge numbers of poor women and children was proof of their deficiency as developed human beings and indication that if given the vote they would not know how to use it effectively.

Mother Jones' own one-tracked, single-minded goal was to improve the lot of the wage-earning class. That, she firmly believed, would solve the problems of the women she championed. Suffrage was a digression, a dangerous diversion; she did not wish to see it proliferate.

In fact, Mother Jones had little faith altogether in the promises of the electoral system. The real world as she saw it was full of bought politicians, pandering appointees, law courts that served the owning class, and an electorate trained by a press that was owned by the owning class. "I hate your political parties, you Republicans and Democrats," she said in a speech in Toledo. "I want you to deny if you can what I am going to say. You [the office seeker] want an office and must necessarily get into the ring. You must do what that ring says and if you don't you won't be elected. There you are. Each time you [the voter] do that [vote Democratic or Republican] you are voting for a capitalistic bullet and you get it."

Occasionally, Mother Jones might throw her support to and even campaign for a candidate who had shown concern for the interests of working people, but even then she saw that workers would often cast their votes against their own best interests. Then she would berate them: "If a mule had a vote, he would exercise more sense in voting than you do." And she would try to explain, in her own loving fashion, "These federal judges, who continue granting injunctions, are appointed by men who have their political standing through the votes of you labor union fellows! You get down on your knees like a lot of Yahoos when you want something. At the same time you haven't sense enough to take peaceably what belongs to you through the ballot. . .and the bullets which should be sent into your own measly, miserable, dirty carcasses, shoot down innocent men. Women are not responsible because they have not the vote. . . . Don't you think it's about time you began to shoot ballots instead of voting for capitalistic bullets. . . ."

Mother Jones partly based her mistrust of the goals of the suffrage movement on the voting behavior of women in states where they were given the vote before the Nineteenth Constitutional Amendment made it national. The results demonstrated that women voted along party lines, quite like their male relatives. They did not vote to improve society. In fact, suffragists were an emphatically conservative lot. Their class had benefitted from the advance of monopoly capitalism, and they generally approved of the status quo; they simply wanted to participate more fully in it. Mother Jones militantly wanted to change it, so she could find little common ground with them. "Never as long as the women are unorganized," she said, "as long as they devote their time to women's clubs and to the ballot, and to a lot of old meow things that don't concern us at all and have no bearing on the industrial battle, can we succeed."

Mother Jones was wrong. Had she not been so isolated from the company of women she might have come to know it. Even in the gatherings of upper class activist women there was a growing awareness of the destructiveness of unsolved class issues, as today among activist white women there is a growing awareness of the calamity of racism for both oppressed and oppressor.

The Colony Club may have been too extremely rich for Mother Jones' blood, but there were other groups. IWW organizer Elizabeth Gurley Flynn, later a leading Communist jailed often for her work and beliefs, was as class conscious a woman as Mary Jones, and she was a member of the Heterodoxy Club, a group of professional women who met together regularly to hear women speakers on every hot issue of the day. Their discussions and easy camaraderie delighted Elizabeth Flynn. She wrote in her autobiography, "I had worked almost exclusively with men up to this time and my IWW anti-political slant had kept me away from political movements. It was good for my education and a broadening influence for me to come to know all these splendid 'Heterodoxy' members and to share in their en-thusiasms. It made me conscious of women and their many accomplishments. My mother, who had great pride in women, was very pleased by my association with them."

Flynn was lucky; she had support for a late-found appreciation of women. Mother Jones, a generation older, had no such support, not from family and certainly not from the men she worked among. Her life was set into a mold of heroic struggle in which she was essentially alone, isolated by the nature of her work, by her class biases, and mainly by her internalized anti-female sexism. She would have needed a female support system to question and explore these limits to her development, to bare her soul, be changed and strengthened.

She needed a sisterhood, but there was none for her. The women who were beginning to explore their lives as women and seek emancipation, the suffragists and equal rights advocates, had left her class out. The labor and socialist women she knew and loved, and there were many, were limited in the same way she was: loyal to class traditions they weren't ready to disavow, even theoretically. Alone, she could not dare to examine the paradoxes and limitations of her role as Mother. That is her tragedy, because in the end, after a lifetime of gloriously representing Motherhood Incar-nate, the contradictions of her own role defeated her.

When Mother Jones died in 1930, she had been on the UMWA payroll as an organizer in the field for most of thirty-two years, never having held an office within the organization. What that actually means is that this famous labor figure, a national and international legend in her own lifetime, never had any official status whatsoever in her union; she was simply a (meagerly) paid employee. Years of struggle came and went, national and local bureaucracies came and went, men who were hardly more than children when she first worked with them rose to positions of leadership and power, but not Mother Jones. She remained always outside that circle of possibility. Why?

One of her biographers wrote that Mother Jones was not important to the labor movement in an institutional or intellectual sense, and from his portrait of her, one could certainly conclude that she was too garrulous, eccentric, and uncompromising to be a good union official. Clarence Darrow, the great legal crusader, who wrote the preface to her 1925 autobiography said, rather patronizingly I think, that she was a woman of action, not a thinking type, not given to interest in reading, philosophy, and compromise.

That does not seem to jibe with what one finds in her collected speeches and writings. One sees, for instance, frequent references to the issue of ownership of the means of production and other basic considerations of Marxist socialism, surely the great philosophical movement of her time. She was an active member of the Socialist Party for years; even a woman of action would have thus been party to much theoretical discussion, like it or not. One sees in her speeches a constant emphasis on the importance of education, quotes from literature and poetry, and in her letters, an abiding preoccupation with the doings of the union. And she wrote and/or dictated the material for dozens of articles in labor and socialist journals and followed the progress of unionism globally.

So let us look at the high union officials of her time, with whom presumably she is being compared, intellectually and institutionally: John Mitchell, with his job as Union president and his salaried status in the National Civic Federation, trapped himself into trying to represent both miners and mine owners, a conflict of institutional interest that cost him his good name in the Union and eventually both jobs.

Fraud and forgery perpetrated by John L. Lewis helped bring President John White victory in a re-election campaign. By the time White's successor, President Frank Hayes, a severe alcoholic, had to step down from the presidency, Lewis was well in place to be appointed president by an Executive Board he had done much to empower. Once president, Lewis ruled UMWA with a despotism that is legendary.

It's possible that Mother Jones might have been too cantankerous for these tender types had she risen in the organization. However, there was no chance of that ever happening. She was a woman, after all.

Mother Jones was not allowed to become "important to the union in an institutional or intellectual sense," not because of any lack of intellect or inability to negotiate, but simply because she was a woman. There might have been other reasons—her enormous popularity with the rank and file, a factor which would have given her considerable power among the bureaucrats; her complete lack of sympathy with her chiefs' interest in luxury: "The fellow who gets fourteen thousand a year and expenses [a pretty hefty income in those days] will hardly take any chances," she said. "In my opinion it is a very great mistake to pay those high salaries."

But reason number one was quite enough to keep her out, even on the local level, where according to labor reporter Art Shields, who was there, the Socialist Party had a lot of influence in those days. Some union districts were headed by Socialist Party members; none, however, were headed by women.

And that was the inevitable limitation of her Mother-role—that Mother Jones could inspire, cajole, wheedle, prod, even threaten from her pedestal, but she could not effect decision; policy was made without her and despite her. Mother could slog through icy streams, dodge arson and bullets, go to jail many times, bring national attention to Labor's cause, build the union's membership and live on next to nothing herself. She would be admired, even worshipped for it—the UMWA's star performer. But men did the important work. Men ran the union.

Today it is an admired piece of the Mother Jones legend that she was never a labor bureaucrat. Her letters, however, reveal the frustration, pain and bitterness of a woman whose entire life was deeply enmeshed with the life of the organization, but who had no direct means of affecting its progress. With not even a delegate's vote to wield, she speaks strong words to the delegates at their conventions, but usually cautions respect for the executives even when she clearly disagrees with them—Father knows best, boys—a woman all too aware that despite her popularity with "the boys" she is there at the sufferance of the leadership.

But her letters, full of dismay and anger, track the doings of UMWA functionaries all over the country as they engage in brutal power struggles at the expense of the membership and of unionism's original high ideals. Clearly rankling at her powerlessness to intervene, she still speaks as "us" and "we," which undoubtedly helped her to feel less excluded:

"It's a sad indictment against us, John, that at this crucial hour we must be fighting each other and fighting corruption in our own ranks—and the enemies' guns turned on us. . . . Use your influence to keep Illinois within the organized labor, under no circumstances let them pull away; if we are divided we are ruined."

With advancing age and probably encouraged by increasing outside recognition, Mother Jones became more openly defiant, opposing conservative policies she disagreed with, going where her sympathies and her own analysis led her, regardless of the wishes of the union hierarchy, trusting her wits and the support of the rank and file to bring her through.

At the time, the union still followed a "we-will-care-for-our-own" policy left over from the days of the specialist trades guilds. Her speeches point to a political growth in consciousness that left the union far behind, her sense of class solidarity and humanity transcending her own entrenched racism and that of her organization. She urged deeply racist West Virginia miners to examine their prejudices, and spoke out for the foreign-born. Hundreds of thousands of unskilled workers were now part of the work force in every industrial area, most of them foreign-born, Black, and in some industries, female. Unorganized, their presence was an impediment to any concerted attempt at improving conditions. "The working class?" said cynical financier industrialist Jay Gould, "I can hire half the working class to kill the other half."

Indeed many foreign-born and African American workers had been brought to the mines as scab labor to break strikes. Although sometimes it was without their knowledge, bitterness against them by displaced workers remained, fueled by a deep vein of racism. Although she fought the company tooth and nail for importing scab labor (and fought scabs as well) Mother Jones pleaded with workers for understanding and solidarity, reminding them that the company was the enemy, that scabs and their families soon came to feel the same exploitation.

For Mother Jones, as for other militant thinkers, it was clear that only solidarity among all workers could bring about the strength needed in this battle, and therefore she was always on the side of supporting a rising up of workers with everything the union had. For John Mitchell, it was more important to conserve the union's hard-won resources for a membership that was already there.

Nineteen hundred and two brought things to a head between Mitchell and Mother Jones. Miners, like industrial workers everywhere, were beginning to rebel at their exploitation, and the UMWA had made enormous gains in Pennsylvania and the other eastern mining areas, in no small part thanks to Mother Jones' extraordinary organizing skills. But instead of pressing the advantage, John Mitchell urged a strike settlement on the miners' convention which brought him acclaim but fell far short of the goal of recognition by the company of the union. For the sake of unity, Mother Jones "supported" the convention's pro-settlement vote, but with a very equivocal speech. She knew perfectly well that without union recognition, every battle would have to be fought over again before long.

Later in the year, she made no such pretense of approval. She openly opposed Mitchell in Colorado in a similar situation and very nearly won. The effort cost her her job; either she resigned or she was fired; whereupon she simply went on organizing, largely for the Western Federation of Miners, a more militant union, and helped in numerous strikes in other industries.

Eventually, she went back on the UMWA payroll, and for the next ten years fought the battle for the miners, and others, in the fields, from the speaker's podium, or from jail. She became an internationally-known figure, lionized in some quarters, despised in others. But essentially, she was a loner, and she made her own rules whenever she could.

Then in 1921, all hell broke loose in the West Virginia coal fields, and she went back in. Thousands of miners had risen up in rebellion against their exploitation and the hated mine guards system, had armed themselves and begun a march against the center of their discontent, the unorganized counties of Logan and Mingo, where the gun thugs held sway. Before they crossed the county line, word came that the federal government was about to move against the miners with gas and bombs.

In the confusion and danger, Mother Jones actually tried to wrest control of the emergency from local union officials who seemed to her to be waffling. Her purpose was to prevent a bloodbath in which "her boys" were sure to be devastated (in fact, they were), but it was a clumsy attempt, and she failed. This time when she left the West Virginia coal fields, it was for good. Despite her quarter century of sacrifice among the miners, she was branded a meddler, a nuisance and a traitor, too old to be in the fight. She never mentioned the Logan march in her autobiography, but she never got over it. Her bitterness surfaces in letters, as in this excerpt, four years after the episode:

"Had he [the district union president] remained in his office when I went to Mamet to stop that march, there would have been a different condition in West Virginia today. He was not heard of when I was facing machine guns and bull pens. He struck me in the face. I have not got over that shock yet. He never offered an apology. Perhaps, John, down all of history the workers have crowned their Leaders and crucified their Saviors."

Mother Jones gave her life to the labor movement and went unrecognized by it too long, but better late than never. As this book goes to print, she is being installed in the United States Department of Labor Hall of Fame in Washington, DC. Also, the process for getting the government to issue a Mother Jones postage stamp has been started by Friends of Mother Jones in Edwardsville, Illinois, near where she is buried. I hope that feminists, too, will claim her at last.

I was 50 years old when the Women's Movement of the 1970s began to change women's relationship to power. Power had been a no-no for women for thirty years, since the end of World War II. The Women's Movement (in my case, its poets and essayists) caused me to welcome my own power for the first time, instead of struggling against it, and for the first time in my adult life, I began to feel—all right, and to build upon that.

And Mother Jones, product of the Victorian age of institutionalized female passivity, what did she feel the first time she stood in front of a lot of tough, depressed, exploited workingmen and with her words, with the passion of her conviction, moved them to tears, to laughter, to anger, and to action? Men held the power, men *were* the power, and there she was in the most astonishing relationship to that power. And when she said, as she did again and again, "Women have such a power, if only they knew how to use it," what was she thinking about? Was she only congratulating herself and putting other women down, or was she talking from an exciting unexplored place of discovery and possibility for all women?

Adrienne Rich wrote in her groundbreaking book *Of Woman Born*: "For the first time in history, a pervasive recognition is developing that the patriarchal system cannot answer for itself; that it is not inevitable; that it is transitory; and that the cross-cultural, global domination of women by men can no longer be either denied or defended. . . . For the first time we are in a position to look around us at the Kingdom of the Fathers and take its measure. What we see is the one system which recorded civilization has never actively challenged, and which has been so universal as to seem a law of nature."

Feminists in the 1990s are the beneficiaries of increasing clarity and strength that has come down to us from at least a century and a half of women's exploration and struggle, all kinds of women. We don't need to bury our foremothers for their faults. If we are to grow beyond their limitations, we need to look squarely at them and see where the unfinished places were and why.

As we move toward the 21st century we dare to work away at the terrible knots of race, class, privilege and power (everyone's heritage from the Kingdom of the Fathers) that stop the threads between our many networks. We are questioning the Kingdom of the Fathers and challenging it with our votes, the gift of our suffragist mothers, and with our presence in the arena, the example of such as Mother Jones.

Mother Jones:
The Most Dangerous
Woman
in America

Play by Ronnie Gilbert

Songs by Si Kahn

Act I

Mother Jones' 100th birthday celebration, May 1, 1930.[1] A farmhouse backyard (the Burgess' truck farm) in the rural Maryland countryside near Washington, D.C.[2]

Before lights come up, we hear:

SOUND

A group of happy people, singing "Hallelujah I'm a Bum" or "Pie in the Sky."[3] (Actual PIANO is heard with the singing.) Song ends with applause and "HAPPY BIRTHDAY! HAPPY BIRTHDAY, MOTHER JONES!" Chatter and laughter continue, as . . .

CAKE LIGHTS up and then STAGE LIGHTS up. MOTHER JONES is seated in chair, next to cake. PIANIST is seen at piano, nearby.

SOUND

MALE VOICE over the chatter: QUIET EVERYONE,

PLEASE, QUIET FOR THE NEWSREEL! (*Bright light hits Mother Jones.*) (*Hubbub dies down.*) NOW, RIGHT INTO THE CAMERA, MOTHER JONES, BIG SMILE, GOOD GIRL. WAVE YOUR HAND—NO, THE OTHER ONE. NOW, SAY "HELLO, EVERYBODY IN THE MOVING PICTURE AUDIENCE, I'M VERY HAPPY TO BE ABLE TO SPEAK TO YOU TODAY FROM MY 100TH . . . ."

She cuts him off sharply.

MOTHER JONES:
What the hell do you know about it? You're telling me how to make a speech? He's trying to tell me how to make a speech—I was making speeches before he was pissing his pants. Start up that machine! (*Makes a speech*)

I have reached my one-hundredth milestone, and I wish I could be here another hundred years to see what the future holds, and be a part of it. Sooner or later, and maybe sooner than we think, evolution and revolution will overthrow the system under which we live, and the workers will gain their own. My life work has been to try to educate the workers to a sense of the wrongs they suffer and to stir them to get off their knees and demand what is rightly theirs. I . . .

Aah, that's enough!

SOUND
Applause, cheers. BLOW OUT THE CANDLES, MOTHER! *Mother Jones blows a very weak breath. The candles on the cake all go out. More cheers.* "GOODNIGHT" babble. PIANO plays "Solidarity Forever,"[4] voices sing it, sounds of people leaving, saying GOODNIGHT, HAPPY BIRTHDAY, etc.

MOTHER JONES:

(*To the departing guests*) Yes, goodnight, goodnight. Tell Mrs. Burgess thanks, she fed the lot of you. Did you get enough to eat—I believe in everyone getting enough to eat. Wonderful cake, eh. . . . Good old Bakers Union! All them candles—you could light up a five mile mine tunnel. Yes, nice to see you, goodnight. . . . No, Mr. Burgess, thank you, I'll sit out here for awhile. Wonderful party, lovely party. . . .

Silence, crickets. Blackout or just a sky.

Lights come back up. Dusk. Light bulbs on. Cake is gone. Banner is down. MOTHER JONES dozing in her chair, snoring. PIANIST playing "Hallelujah, I'm a Bum" softly, sees that she's sleeping, finishes, gets ready to leave quietly, inadvertently slams piano lid. MOTHER JONES wakes and immediately picks up song. PIANIST sits right down and plays it along with her.

MOTHER JONES (SINGS):
Oh, I love my boss, he's a good friend of mine
That's why I am starving out on the breadline.

Hallelujah, I'm a bum, hallelujah, bum again
Hallelujah, give us a handout to revive us again.

(*She laughs, applauds the pianist, then notices the audience.*)

My god, I thought everyone'd gone home! The party's over. There's only me and the piano player. What did you say your name was, dear. . .oh, yes, Keith, Keith Hughes. The Musicians' Union sent him over to play for the party. Stayed to serenade me, didn't you? He knows some of the old songs. . . (*To pianist*) Was your mother in the union, dear? No? (*To audience*) He's a nice boy anyway. Now, are you still here or did you just come? Never mind, as long as you're here, you might as well sit awhile. I suppose you want me to talk to you a bit. All right, just for a while, because I'm tired. What a day! Three hundred twenty-five visitors. Mrs. Burgess counted them. And the presents, greeting cards, flowers, the telegrams. . . .

Now what did I do with that one? Where in hell did I put it . . . . Oh, yes. Wait until you hear this, you won't believe it. (*Retrieves telegram from her bosom, reads*) "May 1st, 1930. Mrs. Mary Harris Jones. Please accept my heartiest congratulations on your 100th birthday anniversary. Your loyalty to your ideals, your fearless adherence to your duty as you have seen it is an inspiration to all who have known you. May you have continued health and happiness as long as life lasts. John D. Rockefeller, Jr!"

John D. Rockefeller. . .what a nice boy. Yes, a nice boy! It was not his fault he was born into all that wealth, fancy professors teaching him nothing at all about real life. I talked to him for two and a half hours like a mother, in his office, I was there. No, he talked simple, just like we do, like any ordinary person, unassuming, modest.[5]

Far more modest than some of our so-called labor leaders of 1930—you wouldn't know them from a rotten capitalist. They bear absolutely no resemblance to the martyrs and saints that I worked with, men who fought, who gave their lives, for no other reason than to make life better for their fellow workers, and for their children.

That John L. Lewis—what a president for the Mine Workers—a bully and a crook. I warned them, I warned my boys. . . . John L. Lewis makes old John Mitchell look like a choir boy.[6]

John Mitchell! President of the United Mine Workers back in . . . 19 . . . 0 . . . whatever! Mr. Mitchell was going to accept the gift of a house from the miners, a house for him and his wife! I took the floor at the union convention—when was it, '03 or '02. . . and I told those miners straight out. . .

(*Addresses the "convention"*) Are you, crazy? What is wrong with you men? Do your wives have houses? No, not a shingle over their heads that doesn't belong to the company. They live in shacks when you work and tents when you have to strike. And you're going to let the union collect $10,000 to build John Mitchell a house? Build your own wife a house, and then you can build him one!

(*To the audience*) Ha! Ha! Put a stop to it, I did. . . . Yes, and John Mitchell never forgot it and never forgave me for it. . .well. . .we disagreed on a lot of things, we did. But he was president. What was I but an organizer in the field. An agitator.

Died a rich man, did our Johnnie Mitchell. Two salaries—union president and paid member of the National Civic Federation. The Civic Federation—now, there was a lovely club. . .the favorite hobby of

Mrs. Borden Harriman, the do-gooder. (*Imitates Mrs. Harriman*) "So inspiring, so delightful, to have labor and capital come together in a brotherhood." She was good at banquets, ran lots of banquets for the Civic Federation . . . . Here's a millionaire, here's a labor leader, here's a millionaire, here's a labor leader . . . a mutual admiration society. Can you believe it? Since when do the robbed sit down to dinner with the robbers—the fellow who brings out the militia to murder my class![7]

John Mitchell would come back all full of himself: (*Imitating Mitchell*) "Oh, Mother, we had the most wonderful time at the banquet in Chicago, we had seventy-five cent drinks and fifty-cent cigars. Here, smell this, the odor is beautiful. . . ."

Well, it ought to be, it's stained with the blood of decent men those infernal hypocrites wrung out of the labor movement! I never sat down to dinner with a capitalist—not even young Rockefeller, when he invited me. The workers would have said I sold them out . . . I couldn't do that to my boys. (*Sings*)

AGITATOR
Lyrics by Ronnie Gilbert
Music by Ronnie Gilbert, Si Kahn and Libby McLaren

Down in the holler where the sun never shines
I took my stand with the men in the mines
With the boy at the breaker, the girl in the mill
I hollered so loud, you can hear me still—
And they called me: Agitator. (They said . . .)

Mother Jones . . . how'd she get so strong?
Mother Jones. . . how'd she live so long? Well,
Mother Jones never bent her knee . . .
Mother Jones taught them how to be,
    how to be free.

You know the washing machine where you wash
    your shirt
Well it's the stick in the middle that does the work
It tugs and twists and it may be mean
But it loosens the dirt, gets the clothes right clean
    And they call it—an Agitator. (They said . . .)

Mother Jones . . . how'd she get so strong
Mother Jones . . . how'd she live so long? Well,
Mother Jones never bent her knee
Mother Jones taught them how to be free.

Some called me Wobbly, some called me Red
Some said they'd love to see me dead
I wasn't scared of their guns, I didn't shed any tears
And I lived to be near 100 years—
As a god-damned—agitator. (They said . . .)

Mother Jones . . . how'd she get so strong
Mother Jones . . . how'd she live so long? Well,
Mother Jones never bent her knee
Mother Jones showed them how to be
    free

———————

(*Crosses to table with tea cozy, tea cup and saucer. Removes cozy, revealing whiskey flask with a screw top that's like a jigger. Unscrews jigger, pours whiskey from flask into jigger, from jigger into tea cup.*)

Now, don't get nervous—this is perfectly legal. The doctor says at my age it's good for me. Sometimes lately it's the only thing that'll stay down. Anyway, I have a legal prescription for it. Don't you wish you did? But I'll tell you what I think about this Prohibition. . .stuffing a rag down the throats of the people.

(*Takes cup and saucer to chair, sits down.*) Don't like saloons on every street corner? All right, let the government manufacture and sell the liquor, as they do the postage stamps. Have you ever seen anyone open a corner emporium for the sale of two-cent stamps? No, indeed. Because there is no profit in it. (*Drinks.*)

One time, I was speaking before a crowd of people, addressing the working men in it. "Mother knows how often you need a drink. . . ." Suddenly, (*claps her hands three times, slowly, illustrating*) this woman in the audience, lifts her little gloved hands. (*Illustrates claps again.*) A temperance meow cat!

"You needn't clap your hands," I told her, "it's to your disgrace. If you knew the workingman's aching back, his swimming head, if you knew his empty stomach, you wouldn't clap your brutal hands like a thug, my sister woman, you wouldn't clap your hands at these poor boys." Ugh—lost my temper. Some women make me lose my temper real easy. . . .

Now, that isn't to say all women. Women have been very good to me in my life. You know, I'm always on the move. My address is like my boots—travels with me wherever I go. And women have housed me, fed me, taken care of me when I've been sick—Mrs. Burgess back there, for instance. . . . She's been looking after me for months. And I love them. Working class women. Wives of men in the struggle—they understand life.

But these temperance cats—what makes them so high and mighty, eh? Don't they know the rich guzzle as ever they did, in their private clubs, where no one can interfere. Do they protest that? No, it's the saloons they close down, the public saloon which is the workingman's only club. That's right. Often it's the only place he can gather with his fellow workers.

They howl about poor women and children suffering because the father spends five cents of his wages on a glass of beer. They don't seem to notice that the family is so poor to begin with because his wages are so poor. They don't raise their voices against that. No, take away his beer, that'll fix it.

No fanatics have a right to say what people shall eat or drink! Give us decent homes and reasonable wages, and people will drink reasonably—most of them.

Now, I will say this for them, the Temperance Union—the California bunch, anyway—they stood up for the organizer Tom Mooney when he was going to be executed for that terrible bombing in San Francisco at the Preparedness Day Parade. Here all the evidence showed he was nowhere near the place, but they were going to kill him anyway. There was such an outcry—and the San Francisco WCTU was right up there with the protesters. So I wrote them a very nice letter, and I told them: "All honor to the noble women of the San Francisco WCTU for standing up for justice." I give credit where credit is due, even to temperance ca. . .women, though I may disagree with them on other things.[8]

And I will say, some of those suffrage and feminist women have spoken pretty well of me, despite our differences. Mrs. Harriman said in her book that I am the most significant woman in America. What do you think of that? The most significant woman in America.

Of course, some of them didn't speak very well of me. Oh, that woman in Colorado. Newspaper woman. Called herself "Polly Pry." Very well-connected socially to men in high places. Suffragist and feminist, she said she was. Oh, she hated trade unions, anarchism, socialism, the public ownership of utilities—and me. Published a magazine full of gossip about Denver society and culture, and she called it "Polly Pry." What a fearlessly honest name. That magazine was only a mouthpiece for the interests of the mine owners. Said she could prove that at one time I was a prostitute and a procuress. I think I was supposed to dissolve with shame and disappear. Where was her shame? Where'd she get the money to start that rag and run it? Newspaper women don't make much money. Who did she have to please to keep her in her furs, her fancy gowns and jewels? There's all kinds of whoring, isn't there. I once started to write a poem. I like to write poems, you didn't know that about me, did you? This poem was called "The Ballad of the Shop Girl."[9] (*Recites*)

The wolf of poverty follows me
Through the dingy streets of Town
So close beside that his shaggy hide
Might almost brush my Gown
And after him thrust the Wolves of Lust
All eager to drag me down.

For body and soul have a scanty dole
from the pittance that I earn
and cold as the breath of the wind of death
are the Sad lessons that I learn

I am one of a Score of a thousand more
who early work and late
and civilization bids me choose
the grave or a degraded fate.

I wrote that in Chicago, just after the fire. Chicago. I wish I was there right now. So many old friends there who couldn't get here. Oh, not that I'm not enjoying your company. But I really expected to have this party in Chicago, I planned it for a couple of years, but then I couldn't get up the get-up-and-go to get up and go. "The Gem of the Prairie," that's what they used to call Chicago. I thought it was beautiful, there on the lake, when I first saw it, and lively. I was hardly more than a girl, just down from a teaching job at a convent school in Michigan.[10] "Goodbye, Miss Harris, God keep you—here's $36 for your six months work." God'd better keep me. Well, that's the best poor girls could aspire to when I was young—teach school or sew. I learned a great deal in that convent. One thing I learned is that I far preferred sewing to bossing little kids. So I took my $36 and I hightailed it for Chicago, thinking to be a dressmaker. And right away I met the most wonderful people: Edith—oh what a grand girl, Edith—she was up for every free concert or lecture in Chicago, and she kept me laughing. . . . But I didn't stay long. I just couldn't find work enough at that time to make a living. So I had to say goodbye to the Gem of the Prairie, and to Edith and all my nice new friends. I heard there were jobs for teachers down in Memphis, Tennessee.[11] They were hiring lots of women teachers in those days, at one-third the salary of the men. But it was a job. I've always gone where the work is, back and forth across the country. Off I went. I was determined to save my pennies and come back to Chicago quick as possible. But as it turned out, I didn't get back up there for quite awhile. I got married in Memphis, Tennessee.

(*Speaks as George Jones*) "George Jones, Ma'am, iron molder, member of the Iron Molder's Union. Might I have this dance?" (*Sings*)

WHEN MY DRESSES WERE NEW
Lyrics and music by Si Kahn

When I was young I worked teaching school
In an old foundry town where the river ran through
Though the pay wasn't much I could keep back a
　　little
To make something special to wear to the dance
In the days when my dresses were new

One Saturday night at the union hall party
I saw a young man from the second shift crew
Leaning back in his chair with his cap tilted down
Still I saw that his eyes were as blue as my gown
In the days when my dresses were new

> He turned in his seat and he gave me a glance
> Saying, *"If it's not taken, might I have this
>   dance?"*
> I looked at him once and I never looked back
> As we waltzed away down the river. . .

Through the long night I never once thought
Of the things my good mother had said not to do
For the heat of the foundry burned deep in his eyes
In the days when my dreams and my dresses were
    new
In the days when my dresses were new
In the days when my dresses were new

———————

The yellow fever got George and our children. Right at the end of the War Between the States. All that killing on the battlefields, and death waiting right there at home. There was a lot of sickness at home—overcrowded conditions, shanties popping up everywhere, bad sewage—well, everything broke down during the war. There was nobody there to fix things. And then this one hot, steamy summer—first there was a terrible attack of cholera. And then the yellow fever. The smell of sulphur—we didn't know what yellow fever really was—that it was mosquitoes causing it. They thought there was a miasma in the air and burning tar and sulphur would drive it out.

Cries and sobs. People dying all around—ten of them in one house across the street. The wheels of the death wagon grinding on the road all day, all night. . . . "Bring out your dead, bring out your dead."

And then our four children got it. I washed their little bodies for burial one by one. And then George. In the good days I used to get annoyed with George, especially at bedtime—him at the union meeting and me alone with a houseful of screaming kids. And then they were all gone. Well. . .The union buried George, with honors. (*Takes envelope out of stack, withdraws fragile letter, reads.*)

"Dec. 30th, 1868—my God! Dearest Mary, my dear friend. Your letter near about broke . . . blah, blah, blah. . . . Now, I'm having to turn down dressmaking work, I'm burning the midnight oil. There is more than enough for both. Come back to Chicago and the friends who love you. Let us put our heads and hands together and we will do something. Your Edith."

So I went back to Chicago. And we did very well, Edith and me. Large fortunes had been made in Chicago on the Civil War, the money came rolling in all those years—to meat packers and lumber merchants and such. Their wives and daughters were outdoing each other with fancy ball gowns. You couldn't make them fancy enough to please them. We could hardly keep up with it. I sat in those new mansions on Lake Shore Drive for four years, pinning and fitting and sewing and beading and embroidering for those women, listening to their whispers about the "dumb Irish" and the "lazy poor." Trying to

keep my mouth shut. It was quite a view of life I got,
inside and out, through the windows of the rich.

STITCH AND SEW
Lyrics and music by Si Kahn

Morning has broken like ice on the lake
Out on the sidewalk the children are passing
Far from their tenements, hungry and cold
Warm in this window I stitch and sew

    Stitch and sew, stitch and sew
    Fingers that ache and heart that is bleeding
    Stitch and sew, stitch and sew
    Watching the children
    I stitch and sew

Wind from the lake rises angry with snow
Out in the street where the jobless are standing
Shaking and shivering, bitter and old
Safe in this mansion I stitch and sew

    Stitch and sew, stitch and sew
    Driving the needle through layers of velvet
    Stitch and sew, stitch and sew
    Eyes on the distance I stitch and sew

Back in the drawing room laughter rings out
There where the "lords and the ladies" are preening
Satins and silks worked in patterns so fine
No word escapes me, I stitch and sew

Stitch and sew, stitch and sew
Pulling the cloth till the needles are breaking
Stitch and sew, stitch and sew
Listening and learning I stitch and sew

Far in the mountains where blood marks the coal
Down in the shaft a fire is growing
Closer and closer it comes to our lives
Waiting for justice I stitch and sew

Stitch and sew, stitch and sew
Pulling the thread till the silk is on fire
Stitch and sew, stitch and sew
Morning is breaking I stitch and sew

———————

Do you know about Mrs. O'Leary's cow? No, it's true—I was there. You see, Chicago in those days was a city of wood, from Poortown to Downtown. Half the roadways were even paved with pine blocks. There was lumber everywhere, always piles of it in warehouses, stacked up on the railcars, ready to be sent all over the country. Most houses had bags of shavings and sawdust—kindling for the woodstove. . . . Even some of those stone bank buildings down-town—fake—wood, carved to look like stone. Ha! We should have known from that about the banks!

Well, the summer and fall of '71 was hot as blazes, and no rain. I'd watch the women lugging their babies from the tenements down to the lake shore for a breath of air, whole families sleeping in the parks at night. By October, fires were breaking out every day. The fire brigade had been chasing them down all over town for weeks. They were exhausted. Then, on the night of the 8th, a wind come up you wouldn't believe, a regular hurricane. And that was the night Mrs. O'Leary's cow kicked over the lamp. Just an old cow kept in a shed next the house.

Now that was a conflagration! We thought—is this an earthquake?—The noise of the tenements crashing down one after the other into the street, we'd never heard anything like it before. Whole blocks bursting into fire, the flames 100 feet high. Embers raining down. Some thought, Is this Judgment Day? The newspapers said 18,000 dwellings burned. All I know is there was an army of people without homes in Chicago—me among them. You should have seen us all down at the lake—jumping into the water to stay cool. Two days of it. It's a good thing old St. Mary's Church opened the door to us, I might be swimming there still. When the smoke cleared, we found that the business was gone, burned up in the fire, and everything we owned with it. Suddenly, no work, no money, no means of support. "The wolf of poverty follows me through the dingy streets of town." What does a woman do? I joined the army, the army of the poor!

It was very interesting, how the newspapers kept talking about the wonderful benefits of the Great Industrial Revolution. According to them, there was a lot of money around. They talked of millions and millions of dollars changing hands every day, deals being made, financiers swallowing each other up. . . Mellon, Gould, Morgan, Carnegie—Rockefeller, the worst. But nobody I knew was getting any of it.

Edith and I would attend these lively lectures on current affairs. There was an old building we often went to—it was all fire scorched, probably unsafe. But oh, how exciting it was to go there, surrounded by hundreds of men and women, as keen and fascinated as we were. There was something every night, a meeting or a lecture. Now, what has happened to meetings? They have gotten so boring. In those days, you should have heard that old building rock with cheers and boos and stamping and laughter. And songs. . . .

(*Sings*) Then raise the scarlet banner high
   Beneath its folds we'll live and die,
   Though cowards flinch and traitors sneer
   We'll keep the red flag flying here.[12]

I had a million questions, and I found the groups where I could argue and ask and be answered. The Knights of Labor was one. Their motto was "An injury to one is the concern of all."

(*Sings*) Storm the fort, ye Knights of Labor,
   Battle for your cause
   Equal rights for every neighbor—
   Down with tyrant laws!

And the speakers, oh, what splendid speakers.

SOUND

(*She mouths the speech, then speaks along with it, the VOICE fades, and it is just her voice finishing:*) "My friends, we have just fought a war to abolish the inhuman practice of chattel slavery, to end forever the disgraceful enslavement of one human being by another. But my friends, I tell you, there is another kind of slavery creeping over this great country—and that is industrial slavery." (*Sings*)

THE WHISKEY RING AND THE RAILROAD TRUST
Lyrics and Music by Si Kahn

If heaven was a thing that money could buy
The rich would live and the poor would die
Ashes to ashes and dust to dust
With the Whiskey Ring and the Railroad Trust
 Let the rich man live and the poor man bust
 Says the Whiskey Ring and the Railroad Trust

 Are you loyal to the Constitution?
 Are you looking for a contribution?
 Here's a little present from the boys in the back
 From the river of whiskey and the solid gold track

Let's have a hand for the railroad track
Let's have a hand for the boys in the back
Ashes to ashes and dust to dust
With the Whiskey Ring and the Railroad Trust
 Let the rich man live and the poor man bust
 Says the Whiskey Ring and the Railroad Trust

 Are you praying for the Resurrection?
 Are you running in the next election?
 Here's a little something you can use as you
  choose
 From the solid gold engine and the river of booze

A hand on your shoulder means a man you can trust
A hand in your pocket means the railroad trust
Ashes to ashes and dust to dust
With the Whiskey Ring and the Railroad Trust
    Let the rich man live and the poor man bust
    Says the Whiskey Ring and the Railroad Trust

    Are you of a pure and lofty nature?
    Do you make a bundle from the legislature?
    Here's some provisions for the campaign trail
    From the bottles of bourbon and the silvery rail

Paper and glue and any old thing
Let's have a hand for the Whiskey Ring
Ashes to ashes and dust to dust
With the Whiskey Ring and the Railroad Trust
    Let the rich man live and the poor man bust
    Says the Whiskey Ring and the Railroad Trust
    Let the rich man live and the poor man bust
    Says the Whiskey Ring and the Railroad Trust

So I got into it . . . and I went all over the place,
I organized everyone, all the industries: steel men in
Gary, Indiana; copper miners in Arizona; chemical
workers in New Jersey; street car men in El Paso and
New York City. And women: factory girls in New
York—made those fancy shirtwaists that they could
never own; dressmakers in Chicago. Bottle washers
in the breweries of Milwaukee, ugh! Girls dressed in
rags, their shoes squishing around in the smelly slops
all day, carrying crates of bottles weighing a ton,
putting up with the foreman's dirty remarks and dirty
hands—and worse—to keep their pitiful jobs.[13]

Slaves, prisoners, these girls. And what's their crime? Poverty. And how about the children in the textile mills—Alabama. Pennsylvania? Here, let me show you this: SHAMOKIN, PENNSYLVANIA, MOTHER MARY JONES, CARE UNITED MINE WORKERS, MOTHER THERE IS A STRIKE IN THE SILK MILLS HERE CAN YOU COME AT ONCE I KNOW YOU CAN DO LOTS OF GOOD COME IF YOU CAN. And it's signed A MINER. And I went! And while I was there I organized the domestic workers, too. Well, why not, who's more exploited than those women?

MOTHERS
Lyrics and music by Si Kahn

There are men of power riding
In their private Pullman cars
With their watch chains and their diamonds
Their port wine and cigars
But the curtains on the coaches
Are like blinders on their eyes
They never see the suffering
They never hear the cries

These men who own the sweatshops
Dressed in their Sunday finery
Sit dining with their mothers
All wrapped in furs and courtesy
Attentive to each whim and wish
Until, silk hat in hand
They bow upon the parting step
"So good to see you, Mother"

Every single worker
Is to a woman born
The mothers are esteemed and praised
The children used and scorned
How can workers be imprisoned
While their mothers are acclaimed
If motherhood is sacred
Why are our children murdered, broken, maimed

So what then of this woman
With no children she can claim
Who will never hear an answer
Though she call them each by name
Her eyes grow bright with anger
Her tongue is sharp with age
Her heart swells up with loneliness
Her blood runs hot with rage

There are coffins in the cutting rooms
Shrouds upon the wooden stairs
There are marks on the machinery
That are not the tracks of sweat or tears
But the blood of broken workers
Crying out for mercy
Each the child of a mother
Each a victim of the factory

Let me cut them to the marrow
Let me weight them down with stones
Let me break into their slumber
Let me chill them to the bones

Every single worker
Is to a woman born
The mothers are esteemed and praised
The children used and scorned
How can workers be imprisoned
While their mothers are acclaimed
If motherhood is sacred
Why are our children murdered, broken, maimed

As a worker—next to nothing
As a mother—nearly all
I draw the mystery of motherhood
Around me like a sword, a shield, a shawl
I draw the mystery of motherhood
Around me like a sword, a shield, a shawl

————————

I can remember the first national strike in this country—1877, the Great Railroad Strike. I was there—in Pittsburgh—when it started. Oh, the people of Pittsburgh hated the Pennsylvania Railroad. Well, the Pennsylvania had the monopoly—there was no limit to the rates they charged or the wages they cut. They bled the business people and they starved the workers—and in the middle of a depression. And it was the same on all the other railroad lines—they forgot about their competition with each other when it came to squeezing the workers—so once it started, the strike spread along the railroads all over the country.

And then it spread into the mines. The workers were beginning to realize that if they stuck together, all the different crafts, and backed each other up, they could squeeze back. Now, you can't run a train engine without coal, can you?

And that's how I come to know the coal miners. They were my favorites, my boys. I like what the newspapers call me: the miners' angel. Some angel! Now, if I'd had the wings of an angel I could have saved my backsides a lot of wear and tear. Riding those one-horse buggies all over the hills of West Virginia. Clop-clop. Sitting in the rail cars for thousands of miles, clicketty clack, clicketty clack, West Virginia to Colorado and back. Cinders blowing in my face. Whoo-whoo!

I started out by selling literature—I was always selling literature, radical publications, socialist publications. That's how I began in this work, selling socialist literature to the workers, giving it away if they had no money—*The Appeal to Reason,* a wonderful magazine. And a book about the English unions called *Merrie England.* A darned good book, too. Tells the truth about the class system. Just as true here as there. I thought people could read their way to freedom.

I took *The Appeal* right down into the mines of Pennsylvania and West Virginia. I had to get past the armed guards, of course, but they took one look at me, sixty-year-old widow woman—where's her knitting needles—and they figured I was handing out religious pamphlets. How'd I get down into the mines? Oh, I have friends in low places.

But of course, then I found that a lot of those poor fellows couldn't read. And I don't mean just the foreign ones. Well, you start work at seven, eight, nine years of age sorting coal in the breakers, you never go to school. And pretty soon the kids don't want to go to school. They think school is only for sissies. One little boy admitted to me he was not eleven years old. I said, "How come you're not in school?" He says, "What do you think I am, a cripple?" Well, how is a person supposed to know and understand the world, and make a contribution to society, when he can't even read?[14] (*Sings*)

YOU ARE THE U IN UNION
Lyrics and music by Si Kahn

BLESSED ARE THE MEEK
BLESSED ARE THE POOR
BLESSED THOSE WHO LOVE THEIR NEIGHBOR
BLESSED ARE THE CHILDREN
BLESSED ARE THE WEAK
BLESSED ARE ALL THOSE WHO LABOR

LIFT UP YOUR EYES
LIFT UP YOUR VOICE
COME TO THE GREAT REUNION
GIVE US YOUR HAND
JOIN IN OUR BAND
YOU ARE THE "U" IN UNION

Come closer, comrades, don't be afraid, I am one of you, I know what it is to suffer. Once, not long ago, hard labor under the earth brought a man and his family reward and dignity. But today you live and labor like slaves for the owner—and your wives and children, too, in the mills above the ground. The owners brought you here from a hundred different places on earth, thinking you won't be able to speak together and consider how to change your conditions. But there is an idea, a word, that can be understood in every language—and that word, my children, is UNION.

SCATTERED AND TOSSED
BATTERED AND LOST
ALL OF THESE YEARS DIVIDED
EACH ONE IS PRECIOUS
EACH PLAYS A PART
WHEN WE ARE ALL UNITED
LIFT UP YOUR EYES
LIFT UP YOUR VOICE
COME TO THE GREAT REUNION
GIVE US YOUR HAND
JOIN IN OUR BAND
YOU ARE THE "U" IN UNION

You say to the mine operator, "Why don't you prop up the mines safely so so many men don't die?" "Oh," he says, "Dagoes are cheaper than props."

Are you a Dago? A Polock? A Nigger? A Redneck? A Mick? Or are you a man? You, my friends, have borne the master's venom too long, allowed him to oppress you. When will you stand together like men and take what is rightly yours? I don't want any favor that's given by the other class; the freedom I fight for and win is the freedom I'll keep.

POOR FROM OUR BIRTH
PROMISED THIS EARTH
LET US UNITE AND SHARE IT
SEEKING FOR JUSTICE
HERE IN THIS WORLD
WE SHALL ONE DAY INHERIT

One night, I was walking with a comrade up the mountain to where we'd called a meeting. The night was dark, no moon, no stars. I said, "John, I wonder if anyone's going to come out tonight." Then we got to the top, and saw the people coming, their lanterns moving up the trails like hundreds of little stars. I said to John, "There's the star of hope, the star of the future, the star of the true miner. That star's going to light the way to a new civilization and that star will shine when all other stars grow dim."

LIFT UP YOUR EYES
LIFT UP YOUR VOICE
COME TO THE GREAT REUNION
GIVE US YOUR HAND
JOIN IN OUR BAND
YOU ARE THE "U" IN UNION (Repeat)

Notes to Act One

1. If May 1st were Mother Jones' true birthday, it would have been a fine coincidence for a woman who devoted her life to the labor movement, for May Day is militant labor's sacred holiday.

On May 1, 1886, in an act of international solidarity, industrial workers all over the world took to the streets to demonstrate for an eight-hour workday. Traditionally, the workday had been sunup to sundown, and when electricity extended daylight, even longer.

Many violent decades passed before the eight-hour day was established. On May Day, along with its celebrations, labor honors those who fell in the cause. I vividly remember a red silk banner spanning the avenue in a New York City May Day parade in the late 1930s. I was a child, marching alongside my mother, an ardent unionist. The banner read: "Remember the Haymarket Martyrs!"

Mother Jones had been deeply involved in the eight-hour movement, of course. She may even have been in the original 1886 May Day demonstration in Chicago that led to the infamous Haymarket Affair which ended in the hanging of those four martyrs.

2. The Burgess' modest home was Mother Jones' last stopping place in a no-permanent-address lifetime. Lillie Mae and Walter Burgess (an ex-miner) had been caring for her since May the year before. Most of that time, though ill and bedridden, she was perfectly alert and saw a constant stream of visitors and press people. (The Burgesses even put up a sign on the road: *This way to Mother Jones.*) On the day of the party she got up, dressed, and spent some

hours with the guests, after which she went back to bed. She died there six months later.

3. "Hallelujah, I'm a Bum" and "Pie in the Sky" are old Wobbly songs, many of which have an honored place in the folk song treasury of the U.S. Satirical parodies of well-known hymns and popular songs, they were actually written by organizers for the militant IWW—the Industrial Workers of the World, or Wobblies, as they were called—whose union-building and search for work kept the songs traveling between lumber camps, railroad sites, rolling mills, mining towns, and hobo camps.

In 1908, the IWW published a number of these songs in a pocket sized collection called *The Little Red Songbook*. The songbook was issued many times over the years, each edition carrying a few new gems, silly or sublime. The little booklet, costing only a few pennies, found a home wherever unionists worked and lived. One found its way into my mother's piano bench in New York City on top of the Czerny exercise books and old popular sheet music.

My mother and I used to sing "Hallelujah, I'm a Bum" together with great gusto from the well-thumbed little booklet, alternating verse after silly verse and practically screaming the chorus. This was quite exciting for me. *Bum* was not a word I was allowed to use in ordinary conversation.

"Hallelujah, I'm a Bum" was written by Harry "Haywire Mac" MacClintock, and "Pie in the Sky" by the legendary Joe Hill.

Mother Jones undoubtedly knew these songs. She was a founding member of the IWW. She parted company with them over their anarchist tactics, but never with their ideals, and surely never with their faith in songs as a great organizing tool.

4. The great labor anthem "Solidarity Forever" was written by Ralph Chaplin, another IWW worker/poet. The tune is "John Brown's Body," or "The Battle Hymn of the Republic." The chorus goes:

> Solidarity forever,
> Solidarity forever,
> Solidarity forever,
> For the union makes us strong.

5. Mother Jones' warm attitude toward JDR, Jr. is a rather mysterious phenomenon. Her longtime bitter enmity toward the Rockefellers, Senior and Junior, was well known. She had organized for a decade in the hellish mining camps of the Rockefeller-controlled Colorado Fuel and Iron Company, and knew firsthand the effect on the miners and their families of the company's unparalleled managerial ruthlessness. The accident rate, for instance, was enormous—three or four times higher than elsewhere in the industry. To her, as to most union people, the Rockefellers were the Darth Vaders of Monopoly Capital.

But in 1915, she and JDR, Jr. were opposing witnesses before a Congressional commission on the causes of labor strife, and he invited her to his office afterwards to tell him what she personally knew about the situation in his mines. She emerged from that meeting saying she had "misjudged that young man sadly." Apparently, the lad with the diffident air convinced her, if not the commission, that he knew nothing of the conditions she described. Actually, there was much evidence in a later session to show that his claim of personal ignorance in the Colorado situation was a tissue of lies, but Mother Jones could not or would not abandon her conviction that he was a misunderstood young fellow with a good heart who had simply been brought up wrong.

6. Mother Jones, like most union people, thought highly of John Mitchell in the early years of the UMWA, but his growing conservatism, his wish to be conciliatory with the owners in situations where militancy would have served the miners better turned her off to him.

John L. Lewis was another matter. The brutality with which he rose to power in the union and made himself absolute ruler, purging any and all opposition, could perhaps only have been exercised in an organization rife with dissension and corruption. Mother Jones, sick at heart, watched this process through the 1920s. By the time of her 100th birthday celebration, union membership had fallen three quarters to nine tenths below its former level, and she had pretty much given up hope for the organization and for the workers it represented.

UMWA's story was far from over, however. A few years later, the union not only recovered and rebuilt itself, but John L. Lewis himself led a militant movement that would radically change the character of unionism in the U.S. for the next decade, a change Mother Jones would have heartily appreciated. Unfortunately, she did not live to see it.

7. The National Civic Federation claimed to bring together three sectors of American life: Business, Labor, and something called "The Public," the stated aim being to lessen strife between Labor and Business. The membership consisted of industrialists (or their representatives), extremely conservative labor

leaders, and prominent citizens like Mrs. Harriman, who just happened to have close ties to industrial and banking interests (the J.P. Morgan family, in her case.) Actually, the three groups were united on one principle which outweighed any possible differences: they were all enemies of militant aggressive unionism, whose partisan Mother Jones had ever been.

Young Mrs. Harriman, social and fun-loving, was in fact also quite idealistic. She took the stated aims of the Civic Federation much to heart in her own way. However, Mother Jones took a jaundiced view of her good intentions and democratic guest lists. Imitating Mrs. Harriman at a miners' convention, Mother Jones sputtered: "And then [she] will say, `How deah! I get such an inspiration!' Inspiration from a couple of old labor scavengers! What do you think of such rot!"

This report from a newspaper society column was the sort of thing that set Mother Jones' teeth on edge: ". . . waiters in gorgeous livery served, pretty misses in costumes, led by Miss Edith Harriman, posed in quaint tableaux . . . Mrs. Harriman presided at the center table. To the right and left of her sat Mitchell and Healy. . .," etc.

8. Prohibition was the law of the land during the last ten years of Mother Jones' life. Her view of it followed her general outlook: Prohibition was a conspiracy of businessmen, sanctimonious sky pilots, and do-gooders who were robbing the working class once more. Mother Jones enjoyed sitting down with "the boys" for a drink and rejected moralistic views on the "evils of drink." Nevertheless, she could not have been unaware that alcohol was a serious problem in workers' lives. At conventions, she teased the delegates about their thirst, and more seriously,

admonished them to take care of their business "like men" and do their drinking later. At critical times in the course of strikes, she urged the women, "For god's sake, keep the men away from the saloon."

9. This is a condensed version of several revisions of the poem in Mother Jones' handwriting in a copybook found among her belongings.

10. Mary Harris apparently completed only one year of the two year program at the Toronto Normal School, which she attended for teacher training. That was enough to qualify her for most teaching positions in those days. In fact, her training compared well with that of most teachers. Most ordinary schools did not require much more of a teacher than that she read and write and maintain discipline.

11. Ahead of most southern towns, burgeoning Memphis had established an extensive free public school system by the time Mary Harris arrived. It was a good place to find a teaching job.

12. The tune is the chorus of "O Tannenbaum!"

13. The sexual abuse that women factory workers had to put up with from their supervisors infuriated Mother Jones at least as much as their miserable wages and physical discomfort on the job. In a magazine article she told of having caused a foreman's union card to be revoked for annoying and embarrassing his workers, a rare instance of the offender being punished. Until recently, women have mostly kept quiet about such things, knowing that their chances of a redress of sexual grievance cannot come

close to their chances of being further punished for complaining.

However, even years ago there were limits to women's patience. One afternoon, when I was a child, my mother came back from her factory job much too early in the day, her mouth tight, her face flushed, her eyes shooting fireworks. "We shut down the machines," she blurted out, "we shut them down! He's not going to get away with it, no!"

A factory shutdown was serious business to everyone, certainly to workers in the 1930s for whom a few days lost pay could mean no bread on the table. On this occasion, a jolly foreman, always free, my mother said, with gutter language and jokes, had secretly been annoying individual women for some time for sexual favors. They, being embarrassed and afraid of his power over them—it was he who distributed the work for which they were paid by the piece—had been "keeping mum," as my mother put it. But on this particular day, one of the sewing machine operators had run into the bathroom sobbing. My mother, as "shop chairlady" went after her and heard a story she, too, knew from personal experience. At lunchtime, the women got together and compared notes, and instead of going back to work, they . . . shut down the machines!

I don't know what the upshot of all this was, whether the dressmakers' union supported the women or thought the issue frivolous and fined them; in this union of 90 percent female membership all the officials were men.

14. Mother Jones considered her job to be as much educator as agitator. A goal of the eight-hour movement was to give workers more time to educate

themselves: "Eight hours sleep, eight hours mill, and eight more hours to do what you will." Mother Jones would exhort "her boys" to forsake the poolroom and saloon and go up the hill, take a book, sit under a tree and read (with what success we do not know). Men and women should read the great social theories, should have the pleasure she found in literature and poetry.

I heard this same emphasis on the merits of education from my own mother, who valued it above almost anything else. But with her, as with Mother Jones and other socialists, the main thing about education wasn't our contemporary notion of collecting degrees from a university, it was more basic: change was imminent, the wage slaves in their millions could not be kept down forever, it was in the air. That was what terrified the owning class.

I remember a song from my youth, the tune a marching song, thrilling, heavy, Germanic—Brecht? Eisler? "Learn now your ABC's—you must be ready to take over, you must be ready to take over . . ."

ACT II

MOTHER JONES:

Imagine that newsreel fella trying to tell me how to make a speech. Nobody tells me what to say. John Mitchell tried that in the Colorado mine strikes, and it was the last time he did. I'll never forget that little flunky he sent down to read me the riot act:

"You must not block the settlement for the northern miners. Mr. Mitchell has sent a telegram that he wants the settlement, and he's the President and he pays your salary."

"Have you finished?" says I. "Then I'm going to tell you that if God Almighty wants this strike called off and it's for His own benefit and not the miners', I will raise my voice against it. And as to President John paying me, he never paid me a nickel in his life. It's the miners' hard earned nickels and dimes that pay me, and it's their interest that I am going to serve."

(*She makes a speech to the meeting.*) "Brothers, you English speaking miners of the northern fields! You promised your Italian-speaking brothers in the southern counties that you would support them to the end. Now you are asked to betray them, to make a separate settlement. If you go back to work here and your brothers fall in the south, you will be responsible for their defeat.

"The owners seek to conquer by dividing your ranks, by making distinctions between American and foreign. You are all miners. Hunger and suffering and the cause of your children bind more closely than a common tongue. The iron heel feels the same to all flesh. I know of no east or west, north or south when it comes to my class fighting the battle for justice.

"I don't know what you will do, but I know what I would do in your place. I would stand or fall with this question of eight hours for every worker in every mine in Colorado. We must stand together; if we don't there will be no victory for any of us.

"Goodbye, boys. I shall leave a happy woman if I know that you have decided to stand by our suffering brothers in the south."[1]

And they did—they did. I swung the vote—I convinced them! Imagine—it was a desperately hard strike, yet they decided to stay out.

Oh, I love the people of the mining camps, so brave, strong, patient. Well, you have to be to put up with such a life. For instance, the coal diggers. If you could see as I have how the men labor in these so-called rooms beneath the earth, water dripping down on them, collecting around their ankles—you can imagine what sulphur water does to the skin of your feet, not to speak of the shoe leather. Hacking away at the guts of the mountain, coal dust and blasting powder in their faces, the space sometimes so small they have to work all day bent double or even on their stomachs. Fifteen, sixteen hour shifts the diggers put in before the union came, never having the privilege of seeing their children's faces awake. What a life, between accidents and slow suffocation from black lung—a short lifetime of suffering, if they're lucky.

I said this to a man once—ha, a man!—no, a mine superintendent. "Suffer?" he said, "they don't suffer. They don't even speak English!"

That John Mitchell, he was a miner before he was union president. How could he do it to those miners in the southern fields? You know what he did? You won't believe this. After the vote I left Colorado, and in a few days, he ordered another convention and got the vote changed. Left those poor devils in the south out on their own. Before you knew it, they were evicted from their shacks, out on the side of the mountain for the winter, rags around their feet, hungry as wolves—men, women, children. But they wouldn't give up—not until they were literally starving would they be driven back into the mine, those that weren't blacklisted altogether.

Those mine camp women, they're heroic, you know. Now, I've been in strikes all my life, and I'll tell you this: every strike that's won is won by women. The women are the ones who bear the brunt of a strike, always. In the mining country, living in tents, food scarce, hardly an hour to call their own what with children running wild and men underfoot all day. But when the men get discouraged, it's the women who stand up with their babies in their arms. (*She imitates Italian accent*) NO MAN O' MINE A GONNA GO BACK A TO WORK UNTIL THE STRIKE SHE'S A WON! Now when those women get their dander up, look out!

Oh! Did I tell you? No I didn't—oh! Let me tell you about the Women's Army.

See, we were getting close to having the Pennsylvania coal fields organized back in 1899. But there was one key place, a link in the chain—Arnot, Pennsylvania. The company kept bringing in scabs and the men were getting discouraged. Late one night, I met with the women and we made a plan to leave the babies home with the men the next day and go up to the mine ourselves in a great pack, armed with mops and brooms and such, and see what we could do about the scabs. Well, we cleaned them out! When we got through with them even the mules didn't want to be scabs and come running down the mountain, followed by the scabs, followed by us with our mops and brooms.

Oh, that was a great organizing tool, the Women's Army. At one time, we had an army of several thousand, and a little musical band. We marched fifteen miles over the mountain from the town of MacAdoo, which was thoroughly union, to the unorganized town of Coaldale. Coaldale was guarded day and night to keep organizers out.

Sometime in the night, we met a patrol of militia. "I'll charge bayonets if you don't go back," says the Colonel, or whatever he was. "Who—against us, Colonel?" says I, and his men fell apart laughing at us—this funny army of women in kitchen aprons with brooms and dishpans, and a brass band. Well, what were they going to do with us in the middle of the night on the top of the mountain? They held us awhile and then they let us pass, the fools. When morning came, there we were down in Coaldale, just as the men were going to work, beating on our pans and yelling, "Join the Union, join the Union!" You couldn't keep them from joining—five thousand pledges! That's all those Coaldale men needed, a little female encouragement.

We got so enthusiastic that we organized the streetcar men to refuse to haul scabs for the coal company. And then, as there were no other groups to organize, we marched ourselves home over the mountains, beating on our pans and singing patriotic songs. You can always make a stir with a bunch of women and a band.

I loved those coal camp women, wherever they came from—Italy, Ireland, Poland, Hungaria, or the hills of West Virginia for five generations—women who'll scratch out a meal from next to nothing and share whatever it is with you, who'll find a song somewhere in the day's drudgery! I'd curl up with their kids for my night's rest, and I'd hear them singing the hungry little things to sleep, these women who asked for so little in life and who received even less. (*Sings*)

Mother Jones

TARPAPER SHACKS
Lyrics and music by Si Kahn

There's a tarpaper shack down in the valley
Where I have lived these thirty years
But it will be my home no longer
When I leave this vale of tears.

There ain't no tarpaper shacks in Heaven
The Lord will be my landlord there
The creeks are bright and clean in Heaven
There ain't no coal dust in the air.

My children they go cold and hungry
My husband he is sick and tired
There ain't no food to cook for dinner
There ain't no coal to make a fire.

In the dark outside my window
I can see their carbides shine
From the graveyard the souls of miners
Walk with my husband to the mine.

There ain't no tarpaper shacks in Heaven
The Lord will be my landlord there
The creeks are bright and clean in Heaven
There ain't no coal dust in the air.

———————

Women have such a power, you know. But they
don't know how to use it, most of them. Temperance!
Charity! Suffrage. . . . Oh, I see that upsets you. Well,
here we are, 1930, ten years since the passage of the
Nineteenth Amendment, has anything changed for

the working man or woman? On the contrary, when has it been worse? Elections! The government isn't in Washington, it's in Wall Street, and that gang of pirates plunders the land and the people at will.

Now the suffrage women were sincere, I'll give them that, but they didn't have my class in mind when they fought for the vote, most of them. Give us the vote, they said, we'll defeat the undesirable voters.

Now, that Mrs. Harriman, the one that was so busy making banquets for overpaid union officials— she actually had possibilities. Congress wanted to find out why all the labor strife. Such a mystery. So they put a commission together to study the situation and make recommendations, the Commission on Industrial Labor, and she was on it, Mrs. Harriman. Well, it was the first time we were getting a chance to tell our side of the story. So, I wanted to find out once and for all if Mrs. Harriman was friend or foe, so I went to see her in her house in Washington.

The maid showed me into the garden. It was a lovely garden, to sit there you would never know there was strife in the world. Birds flew from tree to bush, and a little wind chime tinkled. I thought about the women I worked among, what any of one of them would have given for an hour in such a place. So Mrs. Harriman comes down, very surprised. "Why, Mother Jones, what a pleasure, welcome, welcome welcome—what can I do for you?" So I decided, I'll come right out with it.

"Mrs. Harriman, I came to find out what you're like, if you're good for anything. There you are sitting on the Commission, a very influential position. You're hearing testimony about conditions in this country you never suspected. Am I right?" She says, "Yes."

"And you're going to be making recommendations when it's all over, right?" She says, "Yes, that's right."

"And you've told the newspapers that you wish to ease some of the suffering that you're seeing. Am I right?"

"Oh yes, Mother Jones, yes, that is right."

"Well," I says, "that's very commendable. But I wonder what you mean by help. It's not charity you want them to give us?"

You see, it has been my experience that when rich women get interested in the poor it's out of pity. It makes them sad to see the poor suffer, and it makes them feel good to help weaker creatures. But the question is, how do they feel when the poor get together to build their own strength, to help themselves? That's what a union is about. Will they support us then? And that's what I asked her.

"Why, Mother Jones," she says, "I consider it the sacred duty of those who have more to give to those who have less. And so do many of my friends. I belong to a woman's club, the Colony Club—in fact, I started it. Many of our members feel it is a matter of personal honor to get their husbands' money into good charitable works. You wouldn't want that to stop, would you?"

"No, no, of course not," I said. "But you know, Mrs. Harriman, some of those husbands give with one hand and smash with the other. Now, you're an intelligent woman; I can see you're sincere." I told her that. "Surely you can see by now that workers are sometimes forced to strike, as in the present Colorado situation."

"Yes," she said, "I have taken that position at times. You know, Mother Jones, I may have to leave the Civic Federation. They've grown unhappy with me."

"Oh, is that so?" says I.

"Yes, they say that my work with the Labor Commission has made me radical."

"Do they, now. And you've stood up to them, have you?"

"Yes, I have."

"Good for you, Mrs. Harriman! Well now, this Colorado strike being so hard on the women and children—they're literally starving out there—maybe you could raise some money for them at the Colony Club. Of course, I don't know what your friends will think of you, taking up the cause of the workers in this strike. But you never get anywhere, do you, if you worry about what people think of you?"

Well, I must have touched something there, because she blushed up to the roots of her hair. Then she got all excited, and she says to me, "I'll tell you what, Mother Jones, you come and talk to them. I'll arrange it. I'll get a crowd of women. We'll have a banquet. There'll be wonderful women there," she says. "I know when they hear you speak, as I have, they'll give you their hearts—and their money. Will you do it?" I said, "I will."[2]

SONG/SPEAK: THE COLONY CLUB RAG

(*End of speech at the Colony Club*)
    . . . And so I want to say to you good women who have done so much for the people of shattered Belgium, can you do less for the desperate, starving women and children of Colorado?
    Thank you. I'll take questions now.

(*She does all the voices*)
#1   Mother Jones, it's getting late
        And what I've come to hear you state is
        What is your position on The Vote?

#2   Yes, Mother Jones,
        Considering what you have said tonight
        The vote in women's loving hands
        Would be an instrument for change
        And help you win your fight.

M.J.   (*Like an aside*)
        The vote, the vote, the Female Vote
        If anything will get my goat
        It's "What is my position on the Vote?"

        In Colorado this very day
           Women vote and have their say
           And whom do they elect?
           The one who has the biggest smile,
           The one who tells the biggest lie,
           I challenge you to show that's incorrect.

Now look, I know that you mean well
   But you should be out raising hell
   To get the courts to let us organize
   I've never had a vote, you know
   I raise hell every place I go
   It makes the people open up their eyes.

#1   Mother Jones, are you anti-woman suffrage?

M.J.   I'm not anti anything that will bring freedom
      to my class.

#2   But Mother Jones, we're not the same
     We feel that it's a crying shame
     We women are like children to our husbands
       and our masters
     We are governed by men, but we don't elect
       them
     We resent our position as their pets and mere
       delights
     Mother Jones, what's your stand on Women's
       Rights?

M.J.   Rights, rights, women's rights
      If anything will make me fight
      It's answering the rich on Women's Rights.

A woman has a right to have a house
   that's tight and free from rats
And children have a right to eat
   three times a day,
   and more than that

And men have rights to work
    and not get killed or maimed,
    and bring home pay
And have an hour to see their kids
    and rest their bones
    on Sunday (and have a beer when they're
    thirsty) . . .

(*Spoken*) Then, up stands this bejewelled cat, fingers all in rings, pearls across her bosom: "She's an anti! I'm not going to sit here and listen to any more of this. Ladies, who is with me?" That's all I needed, I couldn't stop myself. "Ladies! Look, whatever your belief, whatever your fight, don't be a lady. Ladies are parlor parasites. (*"Follows" them with her voice as they run out.*) God makes women, the Rockefellers make ladies, and keep them busy with Charity and Temperance and . . . (*Door slam!*) . . . Suffrage!

I didn't make many friends that night for the starving women and children of Colorado.

I don't know what it is
when I'm around these wealthy women
I see their jewels, they see my rags,
They can't hear me, I can't hear them . . . .

(*To pianist*) I'm feeling a bit tired, dear. Why don't you play something for us. (*PIANIST plays "Solidarity Forever" and she sings the chorus softly, gently encouraging the audience to sing it with her.*)

SOLIDARITY FOREVER
SOLIDARITY FOREVER
SOLIDARITY FOREVER
FOR THE UNION MAKES US STRONG.

Telegrams from all over the world today. France, England, Canada, Mexico, of course. (*Takes out telegram, tries to read*) Trabajadores Mexican-os . . . something, something . . . Solidari-dad. I can't read it very well, it's in Mexican. I was at Mexico several times. They invited me down there. You see, some time back I got some Mexican revolutionists out of our jails. The police were going to send them back to Mexico where they'd be killed by that tyrant Diaz. I went straight to President Taft and I got those fellas released.

So, when they won their revolution down there in Mexico they sent for me. When I got there they pelted me with flowers, put me in an open car, flowers up to my chin, the reporter said all they could see was my white hair. Madre Juanita, they called me. They'd have given me land, taken care of me the rest of my life, they said so. I couldn't take pay for what I did. I always understood we'd better help them achieve a decent life down there, with decent wages, or starving Mexicans would be breaking strikes up here, another source of slave labor for the capitalists.

President Taft was quite a nice fellow. "Mrs. Jones," he says to me, "I'm afraid if I put the power of reprieve in your hands there'd be nobody left in the jails." I told him, "Don't worry, Mr. President, it's true I'd let out a lot of prisoners, but there's some high-class burglars out here that I'd see inside in a minute."

The fact is, I don't believe in prisons, and I told the President . . . if this country spent half the money it spends on jails educating people, giving them a chance, we'd have a far higher civilization and there'd be little need for prisons. On the other hand, as far as I'm concerned jail is no disgrace if your cause is just.

They usually threw me in jail for holding meetings on company property—defying court injunctions. Injunctions! This company lawyer said in an interview, "We threw the police at them, we threw the armed guards at them, and the miners fought back and won. Then we got the injunction—and we had them!" Well, not quite. Not always. (*Sings*)

JAIL CAN'T HOLD MY BODY DOWN
Lyrics and music by Si Kahn

Standing on the picket line hooting at the scabs
Sheriff said he'd teach us right from wrong
'Thirty dollars, thirty days!' that judge
 he wrote it down
Sitting in that narrow cell we sang
 the whole night long

  Jail can't hold my body down
  Chains can't turn my soul around
  I'm singing through the bars
  Flying free among the moon and stars
  Jail can't hold my body down

Locked there in that prison with our children
    by our side
We sang just like a cat let loose in hell
Slept all day and sang all night, that judge
    just lay awake
Sent down for the sheriff and he opened
    up that cell

      Jail can't hold my body down
      Chains can't turn my soul around
      I'm singing through the bars
      Flying free among the moon and stars
      Jail can't hold my body down

Have you known the freedom of voices
    joined together
Have you felt the power in that sound
While there is a soul in prison I shall not be free
While there is a song in prison we shall not be
    bound

      Jail can't hold my body down
      Chains can't turn my soul around
      I'm singing through the bars
      Flying free among the moon and stars
      Jail can't hold my body down
      Jail can't hold my body down

      Jail can't hold my body down

    Between the injunctions and the hired gunmen, it was quite exciting at times. One time a Mr. West, a reporter for the *Baltimore Sun* come down to interview me when I was organizing the Paint Creek district of West Virginia, so I took him along to Wineberg, where I'd called a meeting. We were walking up on the railroad bed, counting ties, because we weren't allowed to use the public road. The injunction said we weren't to hold a meeting near a working mine. Well, the public road was near a working mine. We come around the bend, and sure enough, there's guards on the track.

"My God," says West, "is that a Gatling gun?"

"That's right, Mr. West, there's law and order for you—injunctions for the company, machine gun bullets for the workers."

I says, "Come on Mr. West, we'll have to walk the creek, there's no other way. It's going to be a wet meeting tonight." And so it was. The miners stood in the water with me with their trouser legs rolled up and their shoes in their hands and took the obligation to the union.

One of the boys said, afterwards, "You must be tired, Mother, wouldn't you like to come up to my place and have a cup of tea?" And one of these detectives standing up on the bank with his hand on his gun calls out, "She can't go to your house, it's private property."

"I pay rent," the miner says.

"Private property all the same. She steps out of the creek, I'll arrest her for trespassing."

Mr. West got an eyeful.

I hate government by injunction. And government by militia. West Virginia and Colorado, the worst. One time, the governor of Colorado, that little company lap dog, he wanted me out of the state. So he sends the militia after me, six men with bayonets after one little old lady. Throws me into a military bastille with soldiers guarding all around. Going to try me in a military court—for a civil matter and while the civil courts are open for business. Now, can you believe it?

I'm not afraid of the courts, never was. I well remember the first time I got hauled into a court, a civil court. Nineteen—0—2, Parkersburg, West Virginia. What was I. . . close to seventy years old at the time. I dressed for the occasion, my best black bombazine skirt with the pleats, my tucked jacket with the braid around the lapels, a white shirtwaist, of course, with a lace jabot—and my hat was trimmed in violet moire ribbon. I do believe the old judge was impressed. He suspended my sentence and advised me to use my intelligence for charity work. The prosecutor disagreed.

"There sits the most dangerous woman in America," he says. "She comes into a state where peace and prosperity reign. She crooks her little finger. Twenty-thousand contented miners lay down their tools and walk out of their jobs, on strike!" It was then and there I knew I was doing my job right!

(REPRISE: JAIL CAN'T HOLD MY BODY DOWN—CHORUS)

Oh yes, I speak from long experience when it comes to jail, I've seen enough of them, inside and out. Once I went to visit a prison camp, made an investigation, you know, of prison labor. I was talking to one of the prisoners. "What are you in for?" "Oh, I stole a pair of shoes," he says. "Too bad," says I. "If you'd stolen a railroad, they'd have made you a U.S. senator."

Yes, this fellow had been in quite awhile, though his original sentence was six months. They keep extending their sentences, you see, every time a rule is broken. They don't necessarily tell them in advance what all the rules are. Have you ever seen them working out on the roads, these prisoners, with their legs locked to the ball and chain? Out all day in the broiling sun, repairing the roads. Cheap labor, eh? Oh, how this capitalist system loves cheap labor—gets it from anywhere and anyone they can—foreigners, Mexicans, prisoners, women . . . children.

I spent some time in Alabama, looking into the condition of child workers in the textile mills. The law there says that children under fourteen have to go to school and not be working in the mills. I saw for myself how the law was obeyed by the mill owners.

I applied for a job in Cottondale, Alabama. "Sorry, I've got nothing for you," says the manager, "we only have jobs for families. Down here we like to keep our families together." I lied. I told him I had five children winding things up on the farm, they'd soon be down. I was given work at the looms. My workmates were little grey-faced children, six, eight, nine years old. (*Sings*)

SILK AND SATIN
Lyrics and music by Si Kahn

No school this morning
The whistle's blowing
Children by two's and three's
Tumble down the hill
Out of their childhood
And into the world for good
Out of the schoolyard
And into the mill

    CHORUS
    Silk and satin
    No time for dreaming
    The dawn is breaking
    The 12-hour shift starts soon
    Ribbon and lace
    Go take your place
    Within the shadows of this spinning room

Dressed in her mother's skirt
Too small to reach her work
Worn as the wooden box
On which she stands
Torn from her books and games
She stares at her spinning frame
The threads of childish laughter
Break in her hands

Seasons don't shift in here
Fog doesn't lift in here
Snow doesn't drift in here
When the days turn cold
Wind doesn't blow in here
Rivers don't flow in here
Children don't grow in here
They just get old

———————

I left before my five kids showed up from the farm. And I went to Tuscaloosa and got work in a rope factory, where the lint is so heavy in the air that the machines clog unless they're constantly cleaned and oiled. Kids are small enough to get in and out among the machinery while it's going, oiling and cleaning. It was common to see little crushed hands, fingers snapped off.

I talked to a father near me on the night shift—he had his two girls working. The night shift was six in the evening 'til six in the morning.

"How old are they," I said.
"Six years and seven and a half."
"How much do they get?"
"Ten cents a night, each."
"And you?"
"I get forty."

How do you feed a family on forty cents a night?

The factory is hot. The early morning air outside is cold, damp. Children shiver in their thin clothes, going off shift, their teeth chatter. And another long line of them with their dinner pails come in for the day shift as we leave.

Pneumonia, bronchitis, consumption—you can't clean and oil the lungs. But the birth rate is large. There's always another little hand to tie up the threads when a child worker dies.

I worked night shift in Selma, Alabama. The woman I boarded with had a dear little girl, worked the day shift. One Sunday some children were going to the woods and they stopped for her. "Get up, Maggie, the children are here." "Oh, just let me sleep, Mamma, I'm so tired." So her mother let her sleep. Next morning Maggie left as usual for the mill. We saw her again at four o'clock, when they laid her body on the kitchen table. She drowsed off. Her hair got caught in the machinery. . . .

How the children cried when they came to say goodbye. "Oh, Maggie, we're so sorry you got hurted. We wish you could come back." Not me, I didn't wish it.

You know this Federal Commission on child labor that they finally put together—I'm more or less responsible for it. I'll tell you how it happened.

I was reading in a socialist newspaper and I saw this notice in it: "Comrades! Come and help in this great work. . . . " One hundred thousand textile workers up around Philadelphia were out on strike, many of them children. They wanted to work fifty-five hours a week instead of sixty, were even willing to take a cut in their miserable pay. The owners said no. So they went on strike. Funds had to be raised, and so on.

Oh, by the way, you know who put that notice in the newspaper? Caroline Pemberton. Caroline Hollingsworth Pemberton, a Philadelphia socialite. A socialist socialite, can you believe it? How do you explain that? Evolution?[3]

Well, anyway, I went up to Philadelphia to help out. I tried to get some reporters out to write up the strike—you'd think they'd be interested in sixteen thousand child strikers, many of them with mangled hands. "No, Mrs. Jones," says the editor, "the mill owners own stock in the newspaper, there's no way we could print such a story."

Now, it so happened that what the papers were full of at that time was the tour of the Liberty Bell— Fourth of July coming up and all that. This great cracked symbol of our Revolutionary past was touring around so people could see it for themselves and be inspired. And I thought . . . children are the symbol of our future—I wish the American people could see how child labor is cracking our future.

And then I thought, why not? Why not let them see? Why not let the President himself see? He could push a federal law, since the states weren't willing to enforce their own. So I made a plan and I called the New York papers and told them, and then the Philadelphia papers got interested. Anytime I can get two papers fighting I'm alright.

And that's how it started, the march of the mill children from Philadelphia to Oyster Bay, Long Island, where President Theodore Roosevelt, the monkey chaser, had his summer home. Never did those kids have such a time—we had an elephant from the wild animal show in Coney Island. The newspapers called it Mother Jones's Children's Crusade! (*Sings*)

CHILDREN'S CRUSADE
Lyrics and music by Si Kahn

The President has a summer home
A mansion made of brick and stone
That's built upon the broken bones
Of the children of this land
And while the President's at play
Frolicking on Oyster Bay
These children work twelve hours a day
Risking thumbs and hands

    See where the children come
    Playing on the fife and drum
    Battles are lost and won
    On the road to Oyster Bay
    Crossing the Delaware
    Banners flying here and there
    Freedom is in the air
    On the Children's Crusade

When children go to work, not school
When babies learn to spin and spool
Then gold has bought the golden rule
And justice is a shill
And who will raise a voice or hand
To save this stooped and shivering band
From greed that hangs upon our land
Like smoke above the mill?

We tried to visit Senator Platt
But he left the hotel through the back
Tie him to the trolley track
On the road to Oyster Bay
Oh, say, can you see
Our elephant painted "G.O.P."
Walking along with you and me
On the Children's Crusade

O, you who own these dungeon mills
Who trade in childhood, buy and sell
To make of work a living hell
Where children smolder still
If by some chance there yet remains
Some human blood within your veins
Then hear the cry and break the chains
Of the children of the mill

In Passaic for the night
Then through Jersey City Heights
We only ask what's right
On the road to Oyster Bay
Now we're in Manhattan Beach
Coney Island's down the street
Justice is in our reach
On the Children's Crusade

Land of the bosses' pride
Where children worked and died
We shall not be denied
On the road to Oyster Bay
Freedom will ring again
Children will sing again
Justice is at the end
Of the Children's Crusade
Of the Children's Crusade
Of the Children's Crusade

———————

Teddy the Monkey Chaser. . . . He had a Big Stick, but it wasn't big enough to join the battle to protect children. Children sacrificed on the altar of gold, and he wouldn't even see us. Well, it was a good try. It was discussed everywhere. It woke up the nation to the issue. But the textile strike was lost. So many were lost. (*Sings, as a thought*)

Mother Jones, how'd you get so strong
Mother Jones, how'd you live so long
Mother Jones never bent her knee
Mother Jones showed them how to be free.

I have often been asked, "What keeps you going, Mother?" If I knew that, I'd bottle it and have some right now. I don't know what kept me going through so much fighting. God knows it always came to a fight, and some of them were pretty bloody.

Did you ever hear of the Bull Moose Special? It was a steel covered railroad car fitted out with machine guns and manned by detective agency gun thugs wearing deputy sheriff badges, the same deputy sheriffs that threw the strikers' families out of their shacks, kicking women in the stomach, beating up children.

The union set up a tent colony at Holly Grove for the evicted strikers and their families. One night, the Bull Moose Special slides up to the siding and opens fire as people slept. It was a miracle hundreds weren't killed instead of a handful—a woman asleep in her bed, a man shot down as he ran, a boy with nine bullets in his legs, never to walk again. That was West Virginia, the beautiful hills of West Virginia.

And Colorado? One day the people of the Ludlow tent colony are celebrating Easter—playing baseball, singing songs, entertaining each other, the various nationalities. The next day they were running with their children for their lives from murderers and thugs in the uniform of the National Guard or in no uniform at all—drunken, blood-crazed hired thugs calling themselves soldiers—torching the tents, shooting anything that moved. And the next day, under a burned up tent, in a pit dug for safety in case the bullets flew, they find the bodies of two young women and eleven children, suffocated, roasted to death.

Violence—yes, I have been accused of inciting to violence. Don't you think I know that anything won by violence will be lost by violence? But what are men to do, under siege? What kind of a man is it that won't pick up a gun to protect his family from attack?

So we defended ourselves as best we could against the mine guard system, since the government would not come in, ever, on our side. Just the opposite. It's quite a sight to see the National Guard helping the gun thugs evict strikers' families from their homes. Our side![4]

Logan County, 1921. A millionaire sheriff with his own private army of 300 Baldwin-Felts guards and his own private air force. Loved classical music, Sheriff Chafin did. Chafin and his coal association bosses certainly had it their way on his side of the county line. How many brave men came out of Logan and Mingo Counties feet first trying to organize those poor miners. Or disappeared never to be seen again. And then one day, those Baldwin-Felts b- - - murderers, they killed Sid Hatfield, the only decent lawman the miners ever knew. And the miners of West Virginia had enough, and they rose up in their thousands. They put on their uniforms that they wore when they fought in the trenches in France, and they marched out with their rifles on their shoulders to clean out the gun thugs once and for all—and I was there, and I was with them.

And then . . . Bandholtz, General Bandholtz—he said there was going to be airplanes, bombs and gas, Chafin's planes and General Billy Mitchell's new air force. Gas—can you imagine!

I had to stop that march, I had to stop it. But they wouldn't be stopped. I read them a telegram from President Harding—that's right: "I request that you abandon your purpose and return to your homes and I assure you that my good offices will be used to forever eliminate the gunman system from the state of West Virginia. Signed, Warren A. Harding, President of this great Republic." Yes, I made it up. I faked it. . . So what! If it had only stopped them. I'd have done anything. How many men were killed on Blair Mountain that week, we'll never know. My boys. . .

Those union officials! How dare they call me a traitor, how dare they, them union officials! They weren't heard of when I was facing machine guns, Bull Pens. Calling me a traitor. No gunman ever hurt me like those union officials did. And look at the condition of those poor wretches down in West Virginia today.

I always said if we were destroyed it would be from the inside. John Mitchell, making them change their vote in Colorado, traveling to Europe, living in fancy hotels, *studying the labor movement* while miners' wives are trying to feed their families on sixty-three cents a week strike pay. Business men, business unions! President John Lewis, President John White, President John Mitchell—introducing me at the conventions: "Now we will hear from our friend Mother Jones." Our *friend*? An acquaintance from the outside? Not even *our sister*? Even Mrs. Harriman called me sister!

They haven't got the people anymore, they haven't got them, people who face guns out of love, who'll live poor, like the poorest worker. I was a mother to those miners, and to their wives and to their children—not a traitor, never a traitor.

Most of those miners knew better—they must have known better. They're my boys, they'll always be my boys. I heard—I wonder if it's true—I don't know but I heard there's going to be a new union that'll bring everyone together, at last, all industrial workers, skilled or unskilled. Now, wouldn't I love to be part of that! "An injury to one is the concern of all." I still believe it.[5]

Ah, what the devil am I blubbering about. Probably I'm a bit overtired. It's been a long day. My first caller today—you won't believe it—comes down that road at seven A.M. (*Moves to lilacs*) Carrying these lovely lilacs. Mrs. Burgess couldn't send her away. They're nice, aren't they, lilacs?

You know, I've made plans for my burial. Oh yes. I'll be laid to rest in the Union Miners Cemetery at Mt. Olive, Illinois alongside the martyrs of the Massacre at Virden. Because of their sacrifice, you know, Illinois is one of the best labor states in America at this time. It will be my consolation when I pass away to be sleeping under the same clay with those brave boys.

(*Business with compact, handkerchief, powdering nose*) It's best to let people know while you're still here what you want them to do with the old bones, and not leave them to worry about it after you're gone. There's no use pretending, when you're one hundred years old, that you're going to live on forever. Forever's almost here.

(*To her image in compact*) Pretending, pretending. . . shame on you, Mary Jones, you know you're not one hundred years old!

What, who said that? Old enough . . . ninety-four. . . or ninety-three. . . whatever, I don't remember, I've lost track. Well, nobody pays attention to ninety-four. You have to be one hundred. How do I know I'll make it? And I like to be paid attention to.

And I'm going to have a Catholic funeral, too, at St. Gabriel's in Washington. I've arranged it. I come in Catholic, I'll leave Catholic. Now, if I left the funeral arrangements to others would they have it in a church? Not after all I've had to say about those sanctimonious sky pilots.

But it's not religion that I'm against—Jesus was an agitator if ever there was one. No, my quarrel is with the officials, the priests, the ministers, the leaders who take unfair advantage of people who have faith, people who in spite of everything—still have faith. (*Sings*)

I WAS THERE [6]
Lyrics and music by Si Kahn

I have been a radical
For fifty years and more
Stood against the powerful
For the workers and the poor
From Canada to Mexico
I traveled everywhere
Wherever trouble called me
    I was there

    Like stitches in a crazy quilt
    That women piece and sew
    Wherever there was suffering
    I was bound to go
    Prodding folks to courage
    Comforting despair
    Whenever help was needed
    I was there

I was there in the depressions
When times were at their worst
But we had them where we wanted
Like a dam about to burst
With fire in our bellies
Revolution in the air
For a moment we saw clear
And I was there

There were times I saw the issues
In quite a different light
And old friends turned against me
But I never left the fight
Though stones were in the pathway
And the road was far from clear
Whether I chose right or wrongly
I was there

On a day when hope goes hungry
And your dreams seem bound to fall
You may see me by the mill
Or just outside the union hall
When the clouds are empty promises
The sky a dark despair
Like an eagle from the mountains
I'll be there

And you, my brave young comrades
When the future sounds its call
Will you be there for the battle
Will you answer, one and all
When the roll is called up yonder
When the roll's called anywhere
Will you stand and answer proudly
I'll be there
Can you stand and answer proudly
I was there

The End

Notes to Act Two

1. In the 19th century, following the Civil War, industrialists created a huge pool of excess labor in the U.S. by encouraging the wholesale immigration of masses of foreign workers who were willing—in fact, had no choice but—to work for extremely low wages, thus forcing down the existing wage scales in the country. Initially, labor attempted to meet this challenge with a demand for strict quotas on immigration, and in the case of Asians, exclusion. But it was an after-the-fact, retro course, and it fed and was fed by the deep vein of racism that already existed in the population.

Mother Jones' speech to the Colorado miners indicates how far she came from her exclusionist days. She had come to believe that only by extending their organizing efforts to all sectors of the working population—African-Americans, women, the foreign-born, could Unions hope to improve conditions for all workers. In this, she was in direct opposition to the policies of the conservative union leadership of the day, who believed that their job was first and foremost to protect the immediate interests of the existing membership. Thus, the clash at the Colorado convention.

2. In an article headed "Fashionable Society Scored," written around this time, Mother Jones wrote about Mrs. Harriman: "She is groping and seeking the light. . . . The hard part of Mrs. Harriman's task will be for her to overcome the effect of her environment, but she is very gifted and has an open mind, which is more than I can say for any others in her class that I have met. . . ."

Florence Harriman's environment had not prevented her from pursuing independent interests. She had indeed founded the Colony Club, over much protest from her society, along the lines of "A woman's home is her club!" and "Women shouldn't have clubs, they'll only use them as addresses for clandestine letters!" She managed the building campaign with great success and directed club programs for years. Her interest in social issues and world affairs eventually led to an appointment as U.S. Minister to Norway, where she served prior to World War II.

Mary Harris Jones and Daisy Harriman were two strong-willed, intelligent, gifted women drawn together for a moment by concerns that passionately and mutually engaged them. I can't help wondering what might have come of that association if extreme class bias and extremely disproportionate privilege hadn't succeeded in poisoning it.

3. The granddaughter of a Confederate general and the daughter of an upper-class Philadelphia family, Caroline Pemberton became a socialist, served as secretary of the Socialist Party for the state of Pennsylvania, and was a leading advocate for the rights of African Americans.

In an appeal to the textile strikers, she urged them to courage, saying that patient submission to grinding poverty, which kept their children in the mills, was neither virtuous nor heroic. It was a statement that could have been made by Mother Jones.

4. The notorious Baldwin-Felts Detective Agency specialized in supplying thugs and professional strikebreakers to industry. Major clients were the mine operators of West Virginia and Colorado. These

"mine guards" functioned much like mercenary armies in third world towns, empowered by their firearms, including machine guns, to have things their way with the inhabitants. Evictions, beatings, assaults on women, and even children, and murder were their stock in trade.

If the miners fought back, the violence could and did escalate into something resembling war. It was usually at this point that the governor of the state would be enlisted to bring in the militia, or it might be that the National Guard was called in. When these soldiers were truly neutral, trouble could die down, at least temporarily. But all too often, the men were led by superiors who were in thrall to the mine or mill operators. In some situations, gunmen and the soldiers could not be told apart. In one of the Colorado coal wars, militiamen received their pay directly from the Company, which had arranged with the governor to bear the cost of their presence.

5. In 1930, amid pronouncements from the experts that all was well in the land, the country slid deep into the economic miasma that came to be known as The Great Depression. Small business failed, to be swallowed up by big business. While announcing that there was plenty of work if only the lazy would do it, and that trends were upward and onward, the lords of industry cut wages ruthlessly and closed down plants. By 1933, some 15,000,000 or more workers were unemployed. Warehouses were stocked with clothing; food was rotting. No one had money to buy. The hunger that gnawed the bellies of the miners' children was now felt all over America.

In 1933, Franklin Roosevelt and the New Deal came to the White House. And in 1935, a coalition of

eight major unions within the national federation—
led by none other than John L. Lewis!—announced
a drive to organize millions of unskilled workers
within basic industry. The rule of the old, conservative, exclusive, specialist unions was being challenged by powerful forces from within and by 35
million unorganized industrial workers from without,
demanding—Union! Winds of change began to blow
away some of the stagnant air, at least among
industrial workers.

In the first month of 1936, the "sit-down strike"
was born: instead of going outside to picket and be
beaten, shot at, and gassed, and watch scab labor be
escorted inside to take over their jobs, workers now
simply shut everything down without advance notice and stayed cozy inside the plant next to their
machines—they occupied the plant, in other words.
Owners fearful for their machinery, hesitated to bring
violence into their own plants; the work stations
being occupied, there was nothing for scabs to do.
The strategy swept the country, from factory to
prison to high school, an idea whose time had come.
Within six months the new coalition, shortly to be
known as the C.I.O., had 2,000,000 members, native
and foreign born, African Americans, and women.

Mother Jones' dream of a militant, alert, inclu-
sive, creative union was coming true. And it was a
singing union! Sometime in 1937 or 1938, my mother
came home from a union meeting with a new song:

When they tie the can to a union man,
Sit down! Sit down!
When they give him the sack, they'll take him back,
Sit down! Sit down!

When the speed-up comes
    just twiddle your thumbs
Sit down! Sit down!
When the boss won't talk, don't take a walk,
Sit down! Sit down!

    Sit down and take a seat
    Sit down and rest your feet
    Sit down, you can't be beat
    Sit down, sit down.

(by Maurice Sugar, United
Auto Workers attorney)

6. The first two stanzas that appear in the text are as sung by Ronnie Gilbert in the play. The stanzas as they were originally written by Si Kahn are as follows:

I have been a radical
For fifty years and more
Stood against the rich and greedy
For the worker and the poor
From Canada to Mexico
I traveled everywhere
Wherever trouble called me
    I was there

    Like stitches in a crazy quilt
    That women piece and sew
    Wherever there was suffering
    I was bound to go
    With angry words for cowardice
    Comfort for despair
    Whenever help was needed
    I was there

Bibliography

Aptheker, Bettina. *Woman's Legacy. Amherst: University of Massachusetts Press. 1982.*

Atkinson, Linda. *Mother Jones, The Most Dangerous Woman in America. NY: Crown Publishers. 1978.*

Baxandall, Rosalyn, Linda Gordon, Susan Reverly. *America's Working Women. NY: Vintage Books. 1976.*

Boyer, Richard and Morais, Herbert. *Labor's Untold Story. NY: Marzani & Munsell, Inc. 1955.*

Camp, Helen. *Mother Jones and the Children's Crusade. Unpublished MA Thesis.*

Cook, Blanche Weisen. *Women and Support Networks. Brooklyn, NY: Out & Out Books. 1979.*

Coté, Charlotte. *Olympia Brown: The Battle for Equality. Racine, WI: Mother Courage Press. 1988.*

Fetherling, Dale. *The Miners' Angel. Carbondale and Edwardsville, IL: Southern Illinois University Press. 1979.*

Flynn, Elizabeth Gurley. *The Rebel Girl. NY: International Publishers. 1982.*

Foner, Phillip. *Mother Jones Speaks. NY: Monad Press. 1983.*

Foner, Phillip. *History of the Labor Movement in the U.S., Vol. 1-8. NY: International Publishers. 1982.*

Foner, Phillip. *Women and the American Labor Movement, Vol. 1. NY: The Free Press. 1979.*

Grossman, Jonathan. *William Sylvis, Pioneer of American Labor.* NY: Columbia University Press. 1945.

Harriman, Florence Jaffray. *From Pinafores to Politics.* NY: Henry Holt. 1923.

Jones, Mary Harris. *The Autobiography of Mother Jones.* Chicago: The Charles Kerr Publishing Co. 1925.

Kornbluh, Joyce ed. *Rebel Voices, an IWW Anthology.* University of Michigan Press, 1964.

Kraditor, Aileen. *The Ideas of the Woman Suffrage Movement.* NY: Columbia University Press. 1965.

Lerner, Gerda. *The Majority Finds its Past.* NY: Oxford University Press. 1979.

Lerner, Gerda. *The Woman in American History.* Menlo Park, CA: Addison-Wesley Publishing Co. 1971.

Long, Priscilla. *Mother Jones, Woman Organizer.* Cambridge, MA: Red Sun Press. 1976.

Long, Priscilla. *Where the Sun Never Shines.* NY: Paragon House. 1989.

McGovern, George, et al. *The Great Coalfield Wars.* Boston: Houghton Mifflin. 1972.

Rich, Adrienne. *Of Woman Born.* NY: W.W. Norton & Co. 1986.

Shields, Art. *My Shaping Up Years.* NY: International Publishers. 1982.

Sklar, Kathryn Kish, ed. *The Autobiography of Florence Kelley* and *The Need of Theoretical Preparation for Philanthropic Work.* Chicago: Charles Kerr Publishing Co. 1986.

Steel, Edward. *The Speeches of Mother Jones.* Pittsburg, PA: University of Pittsburg Press. 1988.

Sullivan, Ken, ed. *The Goldenseal Book of the W. Virginia Mine Wars.* Charleston, W. VA.: Pictorial Histories Publishing Co., Inc. 1991.

Tax, Meredith. *The Rising of the Women.* NY: Monthly Review Press. 1980.

Werstein, Irving. *Labor's Defiant Lady. NY: Crowell. 1969.*

Wieck, David Thoreau. *Woman from Spillertown. Carbondale and Edwardsville, Il: Southern Illinois University Press. 1992.*

Zinn, Howard. *A People's History of the U. S.. NY: HarperCollins. 1990.*

About the Author

Ronnie Gilbert is an original member of the legendary 1950s folk singing group The Weavers. She has had a long and distinguished career in both music and theater, including collaborations with such artists as Pete Seeger, Arlo Guthrie, Joseph Chaikin and Holly Near. She has acted in plays from the mountains of British Columbia to Broadway, performing such works as Sam Shepard and Chaikin's solo 'Tongues and Savage/Love' and Beckett's 'Happy Days.' Over the years she has also worked in feature films and documentaries as actor or narrator, and earned an M. A. in Clinical Psychology, working for a decade as a therapist. Her current project is the one-woman theater piece on the legendary American labor agitator Mother Jones, 'Mother Jones: The Most Dangerous Woman in America.' She lives in Berkeley, California, with her life partner, Donna Korones.

Ronnie Gilbert's Recordings Are Available by Mail

Love Will Find a Way. Recorded live. Songs of tenderness and passion from Ronnie's favorite songwriters, a beautiful collection. 1989 Abbe Alice Music. (CD or Cassette)

Singing With You. The electrifying impact of the voices of Ronnie Gilbert and Holly Near together--live and in the studio. 1986 Redwood Records. (Cassette only)

HARP. Four legends in joyous harmony: Holly, Arlo Guthrie, Ronnie, and Pete Seeger. Recorded live during their 1984 tour. 1985 Redwood Records. (CD or Cassette)

The Spirit is Free. After 20 years, Ronnie came back to music with this luscious recording of classic folk favorites and new songs, now standards in her concert repertoire. 1985 Redwood Records. (Cassette only)

Lifeline. The soul-stirring Ronnie Gilbert/Holly Near national tours captured on this live recording. 1983 Redwood Records. (CD or Cassette)

Cassettes: $10 each; CDs: $15 each

Send your check payable to **Abbe Alice Music, PO Box 8388, Berkeley, CA 94707.** Include $2 shipping and handling per order. California residents include 8.25% sales tax.

To find out about Ronnie's future work, including the original cast recording of *Mother Jones: The Most Dangerous Woman in America*, send us your name and address to the above address.

POSTER ALSO AVAILABLE!

If you would like posters of the front cover of this book, send $5.95 per poster plus $2.50 per order shipping and handling to **Conari Press, 1144 65th St., Suite B, Emeryville, CA 94608.** Or, with a credit card, call **800-685-9595.**